The Home Group

Heartbeat of AA

30th Anniversary Edition

AAGRAPEVINE,Inc.

New York, New York

WWW. AAGRAPEVINE.ORG

The Home Group

Heartbeat of AA

Selected Stories from
AA Grapevine

Third Edition

AAGRAPEVINE, Inc.
New York, New York
WWW. AAGRAPEVINE.ORG

First Edition, 1993, 1995
Second Edition, New and Revised 2005
Third Edition (30th Anniversary), New and Revised 2023
Copyright © 1993, 2005, 2023 by AA Grapevine, Inc.
475 Riverside Drive
New York, New York 10115

AA and Alcoholics Anonymous are registered trademarks of AA World Services, Inc.

Twelve Steps copyright © AA World Services, Inc.; reprinted with permission

ISBN: Print 978-1-938413-87-2

Printed in Canada

AA Preamble

Alcoholics Anonymous is a fellowship of people
who share their experience, strength and hope with each
other that they may solve their common problem
and help others to recover from alcoholism.

The only requirement for membership is a desire to stop drinking.
There are no dues or fees for AA membership;
we are self-supporting through our own contributions.
AA is not allied with any sect, denomination, politics, organization
or institution; does not wish to engage in any controversy,
neither endorses nor opposes any causes.

Our primary purpose is to stay sober
and help other alcoholics to achieve sobriety.

©*AA Grapevine, Inc.*

Contents

SECTION 1   Where Recovery Begins

SECTION 2 The Joys of Service

SECTION 3 The Lessons of Experience

SECTION 4 The Traditions at Work

SECTION 5 Using Technology

Preface

The articles in this booklet are reprinted from the AA Grapevine magazine, the Fellowship's monthly "meeting in print." Written by AA members out of their own experience, they illuminate the many facets of the AA home group.

When we first began to narrow down a selection of material, we were using as a working title, "The Home Group: Key to Unity." Yet in the process of rereading the articles, the need for a broader concept became clear. The home group is where recovery begins; it is where AA members grow up in sobriety by the time-honored process of trial and error, to discover that they can be loved, "warts and all." It is where they learn to put the needs of others, especially the needs of the group, ahead of their own desires. It is where they first have the opportunity to serve others, and where they learn of opportunities to serve beyond the group. It is where they begin to adopt the guiding principles of Alcoholics Anonymous as working realities in their own sober lives.

Because this booklet seeks to illuminate the AA group of today with its unique characteristics, strengths, and problems, most of the articles that follow were chosen from Grapevines published in the 1980s and 1990s. The few older articles are those that state timeless principles or that reflect customs and insights from earlier AA times that add a valuable dimension to present-day situations.

—*The Editorial Staff*
1993

Foreword to the Third Edition

The first edition of *The Home Group: Heartbeat of AA* was published 30 years ago. According to the Grapevine editors at the time, the book sought "to illuminate the AA Group of today, with its unique characteristics, strengths and problems" by providing the stories of 34 home groups, each originally published in AA Grapevine. A second edition in 2005 added eight new stories, noting that the response to the book had been so overwhelming that "readers asked the Grapevine to create a special department on this topic, and '*The Home Group*' debuted in the September 2000 issue."

Here we are now with the new updated 30th Anniversary issue of *The Home Group*, featuring all the stories found in the Second Edition as well as 16 new ones, including an enlightening chapter on home groups that use technology. No other AA Grapevine title has been released in three separate editions, showing the continued popularity of this subject. It's not hard to see why. Home groups are a little like our AA families (except you get to choose your own, an important perk!) and thus important to our growth in sobriety. "I love my home group," Debbie D. writes in her story "Our Primary Purpose." "I listen to the glad tidings and the laughter. We have lots of coffee and donuts, plenty of comfy seats and a spirit in the room that's alive."

From learning the best way to keep a business meeting short (everybody has to stand up, according to J.W. in "Try It Standing Up") to how to make a meeting in another country your home (just keep coming back, virtually, says Tracy L. in "The Day I Unmuted"), the home group may come in ever-changing formats, but its basic purpose endures—to bring all of us together while helping each of us stay sober.

SECTION ONE

Where Recovery Begins

A Spoke in the Wheel
March 1989

One Tuesday night, a lonely confused woman named "Sara" walks through the doors of Alcoholics Anonymous. Sara feels alienated and depressed, feelings she has had most of her life. She is completely demoralized and knows she will never be accepted or feel loved by anyone again. But through all this despair she doesn't want to die. So cautiously she slips in and sits in the far right chair in the very back row. She doesn't raise her hand as a newcomer because she is too paranoid. She is too afraid they will see her and know and then she will be rejected one more time. So every Tuesday night she comes back and quietly sneaks into that chair in the back row because she doesn't want to die and she has no place else to go.

And then one night she is called on and she tries to speak but cries instead. Or maybe one night someone notices her and walks up to her to welcome her. She is given a schedule of meetings and a list of AA phone numbers. She learns she is not alone, but she is still terrified. She learns about establishing a home group and makes the Tuesday night meeting her home group. A woman talks about the things she wants in her life, about how she wants to be and sound and look, and that woman becomes her sponsor.

Now when Sara walks through the door of Alcoholics Anonymous, people come up to her and say, "How are you doing, Sara?" and they mean it. She begins to feel the terror leaving. She is coffeemaker and they need her and now she sits in the front row. She is still scared at some other meetings, but now she has one that she can relax in. She feels a part of something for the first time in her life. Sara smiles now and looks over her family with love as she begins the meeting—she is now the secretary. She sees a lonely woman sneak quietly past everyone and sit down in the very last row on the far right-hand chair—she sees herself two years ago. She walks over and tells the woman she is home and can begin to belong now.

A year later Sara is the general service representative (GSR) for the Tuesday night meeting and then becomes district committee member (DCM) and continues to give back what she has received by carrying the message that she heard in her home group on Tuesday nights.

That is why home groups are so very important to Alcoholics Anonymous. This is where people begin. This is where the spark of service work is first ignited. This is where the AA member begins to learn about the *how* of Alcoholics Anonymous. By selecting a home group, the newcomer begins to feel like he belongs somewhere. He begins to know people and let people know him. He feels safe in this meeting because he knows everyone's story and where they came from. He gets to watch people come and go, so he can actually see what works and what doesn't work. He develops close friendships and when the sea gets rough, he has people who can see over the swelling waves.

The home group is where the AA member takes the first tiny step into making the support system of Alcoholics Anonymous work. This may be by just putting one dollar into the basket every week and knowing where it is going, or by washing coffee cups. By going to the same meeting every week, the AA member hears where the money is going, what the "central office" is, what a coordinator and a GSR do. This gives him a chance to participate in service work. If he did not have a committed home group where he was allowed to vote on issues in AA, he might never listen to anything the GSR or coordinator says to the group. Hence, by getting a home group, the AA member accepts the responsibility of participating in the whole system, thereby keeping the wheels of Alcoholics Anonymous rolling.

Home groups become the spokes in the big wheel of Alcoholics Anonymous. The wheel, according to the Seventh Tradition, cannot be moved by any outside contributions. Because each group is responsible to all AA services, this wheel can roll along and touch those Loner members who do not have the luxury of an AA meeting with coffee, donuts, hugs, and people sharing their experience, strength, and hope. It can rumble along and carry literature and experience, strength, and hope to institutions, treatment facilities, new groups, and all AA groups.

Through home groups contributing to all AA services, Alcoholics Anonymous will continue to touch more and more families, men, and women each year. Because of this kind of support in your home groups, one Tuesday night a lonely alcoholic will not walk up the stairs to Alcoholics Anonymous and find the door barred shut. One day more and more Saras will come tiptoeing through the doors of Alcoholics Anonymous and get on that giant wheel that keeps so many of us clean and sober and free.

G. H.
San Diego, California

Why Have a Home Group?
September 1986

I n a recent letter to a member of the Fellowship, a member of the General Service Office staff referred to the home group as the heartbeat of AA. That made a big impression on me, and I believe that just as surely as we are aware of, sensitive to, and in need of our own heartbeat, each of us needs a home group.

It all began in the home group, didn't it? Not all of us readily identified that mysterious group of people who were trying to help us get sober as our home group. In fact, I am painfully aware that the commitment to become a part of anything escapes many in the early stages of recovery.

Most members of the Fellowship will never have the rewarding experience of attending a General Service Conference. Only a few are even touched by our area assemblies, state and national conventions, and other functions which bring members together from many home groups. Even the district functions might be attended by only a small portion of the membership of the groups involved. To many, their AA is only the home group. If this is so, what should the home group be to the member, and why should a member have a home group?

When we took those first faltering steps to recovery, many of us would have stumbled and fallen once again if we had to make what was to be a miraculous change by ourselves. In my case, the first rays of hope came from those sometimes loving, sometimes cantankerous old geezers who sat around the table in my hometown. A long time before I believed, or even heard, what they told me, I began thinking there might be a chance simply because I thought if they could do it, so could I.

The first slogans I heard came from them. Later, when I heard the same things from speakers at a convention, I thought it was so wise; but it was months before I realized that I first heard those thoughts from the little guy who I thought was so windy and who eventually became my sponsor. In fact, after I got into service work, I thought I needed to go to conventions, assemblies, and forums to get my batteries recharged because things were so dull and routine in my home group.

Now I know that it's not the wonderful people I've met from throughout these great lands who have helped keep me sober most of the time, but those wonderful people sitting around the table in my hometown who loved me when I could not love, who waited for me to quit lying, who tolerated me when I would be part of nothing, and who never asked me to leave when I was obnoxious. Because of their love and patience, I was able finally to get outside of myself and make some sort of commitment to the group.

It seems to me that, in the beginning, a home group is all most of us can possibly handle. It's where we first find a sponsor, where someone first sees that we get a Big Book, where we first see the Steps on the wall, where we learn again to pray, and where we first begin to recover. (Remember the heartbeat?) But most of all, because of the trust that develops through the meetings of a home group, it is where we might first begin to care about someone else so that we might eventually begin to love again, both in AA and among our friends and family.

It is where we first learn to take responsibility so that we might eventually take responsibility for our lives. In my case, that began with the simple chore of cleaning out ashtrays. (How wise that they knew I could do no more!) It was there we learned to do Twelfth Step work so that we could eventually pass on to others what was so freely given to us, thereby assuring the very future and survival of the Fellowship. It was there we first learned about the rest of the Fellowship, and someone began answering the questions about all the mysteries of what makes the whole thing work.

Oh yes, the home group is the heartbeat of the Fellowship. There are many reasons why the Fellowship needs these wonderful groups, and there are many reasons why the groups need each and every member running through their life veins. But most important, we need our home groups. That's where it all began, and it's where it will all end for us. Yes, all of us have also had the job of burying some of those people who passed the recovery program on to each of us.

With this week at the Conference, this phase of my service to the Fellowship, of paying back a small measure of my gratitude, begins to wind down. What will I do now? If I am very, very lucky, those who are doing such a marvelous job of serving the Fellowship in my home group might, just might, allow me to make coffee next week and maybe even talk to a drunk.

R. B.
Neosho, Missouri

The Importance of Group Membership
December 1958

One thing that has attracted me to AA is that there are no "musts." Everything is done on a suggested basis. If there is anything I must do it is up to me to make the decision— no one else will tell me I must do anything. I have found, however, since working at this new way of life, that I am continually changing my attitudes and my thinking. I believe I must do certain things to maintain contented sobriety. One of these is that I must belong to an AA group of my choice and take an active part in its discussions and functions.

When I met AA there was no group in the town I was living in. So I joined a group some forty miles away and took an active part by attending the meetings regularly for some ten months. During this time I met an AA member from Toronto who was moving to Western Ontario. I convinced him he and his family should live in Strathroy. Within a month there was a new group going with two members— Dick and myself.

This group has increased in membership since that day—now we have eight active members. These eight are all married so we have sixteen out to all our open meetings. From this the women decided they would like to start an Al-Anon family group which meets once a week. While the women have their meeting the alcoholics decided they would like to have a discussion group and get into the working part of this Fellowship. So, in three short months a group starting with two alcoholics now has a weekly open meeting, a weekly discussion meeting, and our wives have formed an Al-Anon group.

At the time this group was founded there was a Loner listed in the town in the AA World Directory. He was contacted and within a week joined the group—and his wife joined Al-Anon. It is amazing to see the difference in this man who had almost ten years of sobriety as a lone member. The AA group fellowship and group therapy has rounded out his working of the AA program so that he would be the first to admit he has more contentment and peace of mind than he ever had before. Belonging to a group cultivates a deeper kind of fellowship which many of us want and all of us need. Often we need courage, and we catch it from others who are really working the program. Often we need to know that others are facing just our kind of difficulties and opportunities, and to learn from them how to do something and how not to do it.

Is living for you a tragedy or an opportunity—or does it mean just nothing? Belonging to a group makes life an opportunity for me, life as I find it today, in "this 24."

What I need is something to encourage the best in me while it helps to keep me humble about the worst in me. This I find in my membership in the local group of Alcoholics Anonymous.

Dave W.
Strathroy, Ontario

People Make the Program
December 1992

For almost two years now, I have been attending a very special AA meeting. It is held on Sunday nights, we often have terrific speakers—and it is held in the prison I am incarcerated in.

I can still remember my first months of attending and listening to the various speakers who came from the outside community, sometimes ex-inmates themselves. The nights there wasn't a speaker, the twenty-five or so guys would just hold an open meeting, led by the civilians who always attended, fifty-two Sundays a year, including Easter and Super Bowl Sunday.

Those first months were very hard for me. It seemed like every week one guy, who'd be in prison for DWI perhaps, would say, "Thank God a kid never ran in front of my car..." in the course of sharing his thoughts. I'd go back to my dorm after the meeting and bury my head in my pillow, feeling miserable. Because an eight-year-old kid did run in front of my car when I was so drunk I was on the wrong side of the road, and I was in prison for killing him.

Slowly, I began to emerge from my shell. The Sunday AA meeting began to be a place I could come to and talk to others who shared the pain of their alcoholism and were committed to doing something about it. I was never one to say much during the meeting, except maybe to thank the speaker with a few words. But afterward, while waiting to go back to our dorms and then on the walkway, I would speak to one or two other inmates, telling them a little bit about how bad I felt. I found someone else who had injured a family in an auto accident while he was intoxicated, severely injuring himself also. He was grateful that they and he were alive. Just knowing him made me feel better.

Prison is not a place where trust is easily built, where people share all their stories easily. Our Sunday AA meeting seemed to transcend all that: guys were opening up and sharing bits and pieces of their past pain, deep-felt shame, and their current feelings of gratitude for the program. There was both pain and humor there, too—the ability to laugh at ourselves was an intrinsic part of the healing process.

Eventually it was decided we should have an election, and elect a new inmate to open up the meeting, call for the readings and introductions. I was chosen, and the next week we were without a speaker. I looked at the civilian who said, as he usually does, "Anybody want to come up and share?" I told him I would.

My story came out well enough, but as I got toward the end it became hard to tell, the emotions welling up inside me as I spoke about how badly I had hurt a whole family, the family of the child I killed. I told about the courtroom screams, the nights lying awake feeling I had done something so wrong, I could never be whole or healthy again. It was an incredibly powerful experience for me.

Some time has passed, and I still start the meeting off, come up with a topic now and then whenever we are without a speaker. I have watched as guys left, missing their presence on Sunday nights, then slowly others start to speak up, "fill their shoes" so to speak, as guys gradually determined, as I did, that the meeting was a safe environment to share their experience, strength, and hope. It becomes like a cycle; the new guy who sits in the back slowly working his way up until he is in the front row, right in front of me, raising his hand and saying something I need to hear that day.

I joke and tell the guys, "This meeting is so good, I'd climb the fence to get back *in* to this meeting on Sunday!" Hopefully, I will be one of the "outside speakers" who come in to share—someday. I couldn't say enough about the civilians who come every Sunday. Besides running a great meeting, telling us how we help keep them sober, they have instilled in me a great faith in AA, that it will, as I work it upon my eventual release, help me make the transition back to society.

"You get out of this program what you put into it," is an expression I hear a lot. I'm lucky to be in a meeting where a lot of guys are putting in a lot. Some things about AA in prison are different: mandatory attendance or you're thrown off the list; anonymity being no more than just another long word when your name is on a facility-wide "call-out" sheet each week. But the general feel of a street AA meeting can definitely be preserved in a prison setting. The *people* make the meeting. AA people give people in prison hope. For a little while each Sunday, it's almost like I'm not in prison. *People* make that meeting: all of us who are finally dealing with our alcoholism.

Robert K.
Marcy, New York

Beyond the Generation Gap
August 1985

I look around the room at my home group. About forty of us. A dozen or so have been regulars since this group's first meeting ten years ago. Most of us have been sober for more than five years. A few count their sobriety in days, weeks, or months.

I tick them off in my mind: an eighteen-year-old girl still in high school; a single woman of twenty-two, employed, living alone; a young housewife with two children under the age of six; a man who has lived for eighty-four years, over twenty of which have passed in Alcoholics Anonymous; a pretty matron in her forties whose teenage children cause constant turmoil in her household; a man in his fifties recently laid off from a job he had thought was his for life; another in his sixties whose wife recently and unexpectedly died; one in his early thirties who hates the conditions on his job but is afraid to protest them; a woman in her seventies so busy with club work and golf and travel that she barely has time for a weekly meeting.

Financial standings among these individuals range from zero to affluence. Educational backgrounds cover everything from high school dropout to PhD. From all of them, we catch references to problems, sorrows, big and little triumphs. Often we sense heartbreak or uncertainty over "relationships"—marital, paternal, social, business, erotic. For twenty-one years I have been a part of Alcoholics Anonymous.

Indeed, the traditional four score years and ten have washed me up on the shores of old age. Yet, looking back upon the teenage girl I once was, I recognize the concerns preoccupying the eighteen-year-old at the meeting. Neither have I forgotten the ambitions and dreams that alternately spurred or lured me on in my twenties and thirties; I remember the mistakes I made and the fulfillments and defeats that accompanied or followed those years. I, too, have known the failures and the guilts and the joys associated with parenthood, when one is often too tired to speak civilly to one's children—or to anyone else. I have experienced the frustration and anguish that adolescent rebellion can cause a bewildered mother. And I recall all too well the problems that now exacerbate some of our middle-aged members in dealing with aged and helpless parents.

In the twenty-one years I have spent in AA, I have wrestled aloud with whatever moral or emotional dilemmas I have blundered into in the course of learning to live with other human beings. I have complained while at the same time trying to accept the latest inevitability Mother Nature has allowed to descend on me.

Now, however, sometimes I think I must not unsettle my fellow members by mentioning such reactions as spurts of anger when I think of how short a time is left to me, my dismay at realizing that instead of leaping up stairs and over obstructions in the path I must literally watch my step to avoid turned ankles or broken bones, the annoyances of fading eyesight, diminished hearing, the pain and despair of losing one lifelong friend after another to death.

I have decided to give up this misguided course of not saying what I am afraid "they" won't want to hear because it would remind them of where we are all headed if we live long enough. The truth is that if I disguise the negative feelings that I am very naturally having at this stage of life, I cannot let "them" know about the surprisingly positive discoveries that the disadvantages of growing old have made possible. For example, I have finally learned that in relinquishing some goals because of lessened physical energy, I have been freed to achieve other and more satisfying ones that a deeper and more extensive Me has always known it wanted. It seems that when I was younger, the tiny, willful part of my mind that thought it knew for sure what I ought to do was able to tell the whole of myself what to "go for," whether or not the basic Me wanted or could do it.

Also, since I can no longer dream of all I am going to do "someday"—because from the evidence I see more clearly that that "someday" may never come—I am finally learning really to live one day at a time and to appreciate and be alert to the beautiful, marvel-filled, albeit sometimes infuriating world around me. This is a startlingly pleasant reward.

And if I hadn't acknowledged how finite, how limited my future was, I should not have been able to give up some of the old false gods whom I thought I had to obey, and instead to listen for and heed the dictates of needs and inclinations I used to try to ignore or at least drown out by the shrill voices of the tiny conscious surface of my being whose vocabulary is made up mostly of "I wills" and "I won'ts," rather than of "Now let's see about this" or "Is that what I really prefer?"

Looking over my AA group brought these thoughts to mind, and I see, astonishingly, that there are no gender gaps, no generation gaps, no social chasms here. Starting with the casting-off of the shackles put on us by alcohol, an experience we all share, in the years that follow we deal in much the same ways with all our trials and tribulations, using, as we so often say, the tools our program of recovery gives us.

The girl just reaching puberty, whose main preoccupation (aside from resisting peer pressure to drink or use drugs) may be whether you do or you don't have sex and if so when and with whom; the young man or woman with a new family who feels he/she deserves a raise and isn't sure how far to go in being assertive; the old person trying to budget a Social Security check to include a monthly trip to the slot machines at Lake Tahoe; and me coming to terms with the fact that my Future can at best be only a fraction of what is now my Past—we are not segregated. In AA, as we listen to one another's anxieties and problems, we understand that it's not what's happening to you because you are whatever age you happen to be, or because you are poor, or because you aren't attractive, or because you aren't as smart as your coworkers; it is how you cope with it, survive it, and don't give up and drink over it.

The "it" you survive can be anything: dashed career hopes, unrequited love, crippling disease, poverty, approaching death. Together we face it, equipped only with the vast, previously undiscovered resources of power within us, which faced and conquered alcoholism for us.

So let us not be afraid of unsettling or boring our comrades by talking about our reactions to whatever is bothering us at a given moment; for this way we learn how to live.

B. M.
Saratoga, California

Chill Wind of the Soul
July 2003

I n the days before I took my first drink, I remember seeing a photograph of a renowned existentialist philosopher. He was standing on a tiny ice floe, floating in a vast and otherwise empty sea, totally, absolutely alone. I remember thinking, even then, That's me!

For a time, alcohol helped me to fit in. The first time I drank (which was also the first time I got drunk), I overcame the crushing shyness I felt around girls, and I called one up for my very first date. Alcohol gave me courage when I was scared, helped me to laugh instead of cry, and made me brilliantly inventive and creative.

It forged a tenuous camaraderie of affection and sharing within a family that was being increasingly rent apart by mental illness, rage, and hangovers. For a time, alcohol helped me to feel a connectedness with this family, especially with my dad, whom I loved dearly and whom I wanted to be just like. My main ambition in life at that time was to become a writer, and the writers I most wanted to be like were reportedly just like my dad—they lived life fully, wildly, and alcoholically. I believed that the main qualification for fitting in with them was to drink just the way they did.

But the more I drank, and the longer I drank, the more despondent I became. I tried to fill my wrenching emptiness with more and more alcohol, but no matter how much more I drank, my feelings of loneliness and shame just grew. I eventually came to lose everything that mattered in life. I lost my wife of thirteen years, and I lost a son barely past his first birthday. Losing a spouse is painful enough, but losing a child is unbearable. I lost the house that we had worked so hard for, together with the dog and the car and the white picket fence. I lost my friends, some of whom I had known since childhood. I lost whatever feeling of worth and purpose that remained inside myself. I was riddled with guilt at my selfish behavior and absolutely convinced that I was a gutless, no-good bum who could not stop drinking, no matter how hard I tried.

I did not lose my faith in a Higher Power, for that had been lost long, long ago. Inside my unloved, unloving heart, I knew that I was very near to suicide. At the age of forty, I was a ruined man, a man who now spent his nights and weekends painfully and desperately alone. Each day after work, I returned to my tiny, miserable, barely-furnished apartment (I called it my cell), and once there, I shuttered the windows, bolted the door, unplugged the phone, and proceeded to drink myself into oblivion.

In the morning, I awakened with a head-wracking hangover, sweat beading from my pores, my stomach in knots. Many times, I was still drunk from a night I could not remember. Most mornings, I came to and wished for death. Always, there was the emotional hangover and that chill wind whistling through the gaping hole in my chest where there should have been a heart. I was just about dead inside.

I did not plan on coming to Alcoholics Anonymous. I planned to die. But somehow, through the grace of the Higher Power I did not yet believe in, I was permitted to stumble into a noisy, dingy, smoky room filled with other alcoholics, and something absolutely astounding occurred. A miracle happened!

I listened to the people there tell me how it had been for them, what happened, and what it was like now. I never had heard men and women share their stories the way the people in that meeting did. Their stories sounded just like mine—not necessarily the facts, but the feelings, especially the echoes of past loneliness and despair. I had given up any hope that I could not drink long ago. AA members changed all that with their passion, gratitude, and love. They made me a believer. They made a connection for me. They gave me that very first glimpse of hope.

Later, I heard AA members talk of feeling, in their alcoholic past, a gaping hole in the middle of the chest, and a harsh, chill wind whistling through it. I remembered the man on the ice floe, and I felt the pain of that wind, which had whistled through my chest so many years.

Today, the cold wind has been stilled, and it is the spirit wind that warms my heart. Through working the Twelve Steps, coming to trust a Higher Power I had once denied, and repeatedly asking for help in staying sober and in living life one day at a time, that hole of desolation and apartness has been filled.

Hank M.
Winston-Salem, North Carolina

The Beat Goes On
March 1987

Sometimes, on a warm summer's night, we would leave the front door open for the westerly breeze it would bring.

On those occasions, the speakers would pause periodically as a Southern Pacific fast freight thundered past, drowning out the message.

"Willie the Wino" and "Red Montie" would exchange knowing glances. They had ridden those rails to nowhere with their Thunderbird or Ripple or white port wine. But not anymore. Willie's a rehabilitation counselor; Montie has his own business. Things change. People change.

The old hall at 30 North Main was our fellowship's home for more than twenty years, but places change, too. Last night we held our first meeting in the new meeting place, just down the street, alongside the railroad tracks. I remember my first entry into that dingy old home of ours on North Main eight years ago. Still sweating and vibrating, my only thought was, Oh Lord—where have I ended up?

But the folks in there were happy, joking, clean, and sober. There was "Dave," my old Sunday morning boozing buddy, looking good.

And "Russ." I used to drive him home, telling myself, If I ever get that bad, I'll quit! I can still see him smiling as he would pull two coins from his pocket, rub them together, and remark, "When things get tough I do this and remember the day when I couldn't."

There sat "Lola," our resident old-timer, who will celebrate thirty-eight years of sobriety come February: "I'm Lola, an alcoholic. Thanks to the grace of God and Alcoholics Anonymous, I didn't have to take a drink today!"

There was "Blackie," who used to sleep with his bottle in the weeds in the backyard before he sobered up inside those walls. They put the cigarette butts from each meeting out in back for him like an offering. I remember "Lee S.," who told me one night, "Sure, you have to plan things ahead, but you don't have to plan the results." She went home that night to pass away peacefully in her sleep.

And the little old guy with the accordion—we had to remind him he could sing after the meetings, not *during* them.

So many folks—young and old, rich and poor, plain and fancy—all bound together in our common quest: daily freedom from the tyranny of alcoholism; some succeeding, some failing, only to come back and try again, and some, sadly, slipping through the cracks, lost and gone. So yesterday we bid goodbye to old 30 North Main—no longer dingy but all fixed up in new paint by its new owner, ready for new tenants who could afford more rent than our budget allowed.

Last night's meeting was more than business as usual—nostalgia and reminiscence, sure, but hope and faith in the future, burgeoning from a proven past; conviction that the power in these rooms is greater than the sum total of those of us present.

So the beat goes on. The great beating heart of Alcoholics Anonymous all over the world, and in our little valley city. And there is gratitude shared by us all for the stockbroker and the doctor and God, as we understand him.

S. M.
Lodi, California

The Blizzard of 82
October 1989

The blizzard had started long before anyone in the factory was aware of it. Looking out the security doors in the plant lobby, I could see that the snow falling on Willow Street looked piddling and of no consequence. There had been rumors of a big storm, but nothing had come over the PA system and only a few people had left at noon. It was Tuesday, and in 1982, Tuesday meant just one thing to me. The Springfield Young People's Group met at Emmanuel Church at 9:00 PM. The group met for the first time in March 1969, and there had been a meeting every Tuesday night at nine since. I was very proud of the fact that our group had never canceled a meeting for any reason. The people I grew up with in AA did not believe in canceling meetings. As my good friend John X. used to say, "If the bomb fell in Chicopee, somebody would call up and ask 'What meeting are you going to tonight?'" That's just the way it was.

The first hint of trouble was that the bus from East Hartford to Springfield would be two hours late picking us up at the end of the shift. Even then, we had no idea of the seriousness of the storm. For me, it was still on the order of a minor nuisance. It wasn't until two hours after we had boarded the bus, now going slower and slower, and straining to see out the snow-blinded windows on 91 North, that I started to become concerned. Cars by the dozen had been abandoned. Some trucks had slipped off the road into the dividing ravine and jacknifed. I began to fear that I might even be late for the meeting. But better late than never. In fact, it took three hours to get from East Hartford to Springfield and we arrived at just nine o'clock.

The real shock, though, came when I got off the bus, fifteen miles from home and suddenly up to my waist in snow. The church was there alright. But the doorway was unlit and the windows were black. The lights were out! In my disbelief I actually started to try to approach the door. After a few struggling inches I realized I wasn't going anywhere. This night there would be no meeting!

The only place plowed was the road and I had a long walk ahead of me. There would be plenty of time to absorb the shock. There were a few hardy souls out on sleds and cross country skis. But mostly there was just this ghostly barren emptiness and the eerie sound of snow swishing through bare tree limbs and whipping up the road in spools and whirlpools. The store windows were dark. No cars. The thought of walking home did not bother me at all. The idea of missing my meeting did.

If you have never loved an AA group this won't interest you much. But we were a close-knit bunch and Young People's was something still fairly new in western Massachusetts. Ours was one of the biggest meetings in the valley. About one hundred and fifty people every week. All the chairs were taken and it was standing room only right to the wall. In the warm weather we gauged the size of the meeting by the number of motorcycles in front. It was a five or a seven or a ten-bike meeting. There had been many unforgettable moments there for all of us. This abrupt interruption in the routine brought some of them to mind on the long walk toward downtown Springfield.

One year we had a Christmas meeting and after the Lord's Prayer we had arranged to have some AA kids come in and sing a few carols—"Rudolph," "O Little Town of Bethlehem." But the one that got everybody was "Silent Night." There wasn't a dry eye in the room. Recently I got a phone call from the father of one of those "kids," who is now in college.

One year we had a going away party for committee members who would fly a big jet down to Memphis to put a bid in for the ICYPAA Conference. The house was more packed than ever. All the walls were plastered with posters and cut-out letters saying "Bon Voyage" and balloons were strung across the front of the hall. Some area level service people had shown up just for support. They had given the bid committee everything they could right from the start to get it off the ground and into the air.

Then there was the night one of our more difficult candidates for sobriety began an unauthorized distribution of literature by throwing it all over the room, overturning chairs and just "acting out," as they say in the field. Luckily all this took place before the meeting started so there was time to call the police. After chasing him around the room for a few minutes they finally got the cuffs on him. "What's the charge?" he demanded. One of the officers said "Oh, we'll think of something."

The group's first anniversary was one I had chaired and planned down to the last perfect detail. I thought AA needed a little color and liveliness. I had five singing nuns with guitars just to warm the place up before the meeting. There was a candle at every place setting and the whole thing ended with a rousing chorus of the "Battle Hymn of the Republic." My sponsor was positively catatonic with anger.

One night I called a special business meeting just to resign as chairman of the group. I felt that such an awesome decision called for the presence of a solemn assembly. They weren't sad and they weren't glad. They were accepting. They said okay. I felt very rejected.

Walking along that barren road with no one to talk to, with nothing moving but the snow, I seemed to lose all sense of time. I could not tell whether ten minutes had passed or half an hour.

The main thing about the Young People's meeting was there was a small group of us who had to be there. To make coffee. Put out chairs and literature. But most of all to greet new people. This was our home group and they were our guests. Young people were being sent by the courts and other agencies. There was a rumor we had been infiltrated by the vice squad and were under surveillance. I thought it was pretty funny, but who knows. It may have been true.

Then there was the time the group was split over format and personalities. We called in a seasoned old-timer who had had a lot of service experience. She chaired our first fight as a group (more formally known as a group conscience meeting). That night our group didn't have much of a conscience, however, or at least it was under-informed and in need of direction. She provided it and the group is still going today, stronger than ever.

Over the years in that group lifetimes had been lived, dreams realized, hearts broken and plans trashed. But there had been a meeting. If the Boy Scouts needed the hall, we met in the gym. If the voting machines were in use, we waited until the ballots were counted and had a meeting. Whole groups of leaders came and went. Factions formed and clashed. Tyrants took control and lost all influence. Frightened new people watched from the sidelines until they had the courage to join the fun or fray, whichever was prevailing. But there was a meeting.

I had been walking a long time when I came to a blind steep curve in the road so the truck coming from behind almost hit me. But he pulled over and I got lucky. A man and his family dropped me off right at my street.

I couldn't stop thinking about the group. If the treasurer ran off with the money, there was a meeting. I had trouble sleeping that night. I thought of John X.'s remark about what if the bomb falls. You have a meeting. The image of that darkened church and black windows is still with me. The emptiness, the lost feeling of having been abandoned by a building is one I will never forget. That day remains as one left with a hole in it. If you have never loved a group, no explanation is possible. If you have, none is necessary.

Jim N.
West Springfield, Massachusetts

The Weakest Link

February 1995

"A chain is only as strong as its weakest link." We hear this phrase throughout our life. We might have heard it first from our high school gym coach. Soldiers in the armed forces hear this from drill instructors. It's true in almost every aspect of our society, from the business world to professional sports.

But there is one place where we are made strong by the weakest link, and that is in the wonderful Fellowship of Alcoholics Anonymous. In this case, the weak link is the newcomer. When a new man or woman walks through our doors for the first time, they may feel alone, confused, desperate, and weak. It is at this time that our three legacies of Unity, Service, and Recovery come into full swing. We all pull together to do what we can for newcomers. We are strong as a group and become stronger through their weakness. They become stronger in recovery because of our unity. In essence, the AA chain becomes stronger because of its weakest link.

The same is said for those AAs who succumb to the drink compulsion and have a slip or relapse. If they make it back to meetings, they find strength and support in our unity.

Alcoholics Anonymous is a place where the weak are accepted with open arms. We are all weak links when we find our way into AA. But what makes us strong, as individuals and as a Fellowship, is when we are forged in the furnace of Unity, Service, and Recovery.

Anonymous

A Beacon in the Dark
September 1991

The first time I sneaked my fearful, bewildered self into an AA meeting, I was struck by the seriousness and single-mindedness of the meeting and its participants. The meeting was a somber, pain-filled beginners' meeting. These were the first real alcoholics I had ever seen, and unsure whether I belonged there, I listened for weeks until I found that their pain and bewilderment were the same as mine. But mostly I remember my astonishment as I compared these meetings to the committee meetings I had become accustomed to in my outside life.

I was used to freewheeling discussions, often flying off the subject and into the personal agendas of those present, the jockeying for position, demands for attention and the ego-driven clamoring for the upper hand. I had been a "leader" in my community, and had learned well how meetings worked. You determined how an issue was to be resolved (according to your own knowledge of what was best), convinced others of your point of view beforehand, and generally intimidated the rest to go along. Meetings like this dominated my days for years before I came to AA. I was an expert at running meetings, solving problems, and convincing others of the superiority of my point of view. I had no understanding at the time that this was a symptom of my "self-will run riot." And as long as I was willing to take care of all the details and follow through on the decisions, others seemed to be quite impressed with my command of the organizational structure, and personally I thrived in the leadership roles that I later discovered had become my way of covering up my growing insecurities and my increasing sense that I was losing control.

But here, at AA meetings, was a phenomenon I had never experienced. The meetings began and ended on time. One topic was chosen, each person took a turn, in order, and stayed on the topic. No one interrupted, and to my astonishment some even passed so they could listen to others.

I was glad that no one knew of my prestigious abilities to run meetings because then, at the end of my drinking, I was too beaten and lacked the confidence to do more than offer my brief comments and pass. But I was getting a message: this was serious stuff (too serious to allow for the antics I was used to) and that somehow what was going on here, whatever it was, was working for some people. This fascination with procedure, along with the fact that I was desperate to stop drinking, kept me coming back.

Although it's been quite a few days since those first few meetings, I am still amazed at the aura around AA meetings. I still marvel at the way a group of very ego-driven people quiets down to a hush when the chairperson announces the beginning of a meeting, at the attention when the Steps are read, at the courtesy given to the speaker. No matter what our immediate problems, fears, or resentments, we come to a halt when the meeting begins and focus on our primary purpose.

Nothing illustrates this more than what happened at my home group meeting last spring. A small, soft-spoken woman had begun to speak to the eighty-odd alcoholics gathered that night. We could hear her better because of the new amplifier the group had just bought. Five minutes into her talk, the lightning and thunder raging outside were competing with her whispery voice, and bodies were leaning forward to hear better as Marge told where alcohol had taken her.

Suddenly the lights dimmed twice and then went out, leaving the church basement pitch black. Marge stopped, and everyone waited for the lights and the microphone to go on again. After a few minutes of hushed blackness, the room took on a spooky aspect as tiny flames flickered from cigarette lighters randomly struck around the room.

Still in darkness and silence, Marge resumed her story, while three home group members slowly felt their way to the supply cabinet, found used candles from December's holiday meeting, lit them and placed one on each table. One more was placed on the lectern in front of Marge, illuminating her face as she continued to speak. The three members retook their seats, and in the blackness no one moved or made a sound. We all sat there, Marge's voice somehow amplified by the silent darkness and the earnest concentration of the group.

When Marge came to the part about her recovery, the lights went back on, but no one seemed to notice. No cheer, no acknowledgment at all that anything had changed, except that the posture of the group relaxed slightly in response to the resumption of the sound system that made Marge's voice easier to hear.

After the meeting ended and the room filled with the raucous noise of fellowship, I reflected on the simplicity of this wonderful program. For forty-five minutes, attention to everything around us—the thunder, the sudden blackness, the difficulty of hearing Marge's timid voice, the insecurity of not being able to move about freely—was suspended as we all focused on our primary purpose: one drunk talking to another about alcoholism and recovery.

Nadene S.
Pittsburgh, Pennsylvania

Finally Home
April 2020

I love my home group and invite everyone to come visit. I'd like to think it's the best group in all AA, yet it's just a group like any other. I just happen to feel at home here. It meets every Tuesday and Thursday at a YMCA. I've come to count on it being here. The first thing I noticed about my group was how bright and cheery it is and that there's a lot of sobriety in the room.

It took me time to get to know people. I learned slowly that there were a lot of LGBTQ+ people there who had known each other for years. Some had been sober for 50 years.

I'm a transgender member, and the group embraced me very early on in my recovery. I was so shaky then. I was constantly relapsing, and the group just loved me. They listened to me and made me a part of the group. They kept electing me to service commitments, and no one batted an eye each time I picked up a drink and could no longer do the job. I have since been able to make amends to the group, living and direct, by staying sober and showing up for each commitment they put me up for now.

My entire first year, I sat next to an old gentle giant. I hid in his looming shadow. Such a sweet gentle man he was. After he passed away, I found out that he was a cofounder of our home group, which began a long time ago. I got to attend his memorial. It had such an impact on me to walk in and see my entire home group all dressed up, paying their respects.

Later, I remember getting to sign our group's lease when I was overall chair, still not entirely believing I would be able to stay sober for another entire year.

I'll never forget my first qualification in front of the group. I got weepy and was so moved. These members had watched each other get married, get jobs, lose jobs and loved ones. And they just kept coming and loving one another. All I've ever wanted is to love and be loved in return and to grow old with somebody. Here before my eyes, I could see my home group doing just that with one another.

When I mentioned that they were growing old together, the entire room gasped. Did I really just call them old? How funny. I guess I did! It was such a special moment.

Oh well...I guess I'll keep coming back. They have what I want.

L.M.
Brooklyn, New York

The Sweet Smell of Coffee
April 2020

I arrived at the maximum-security state prison at Elmira, N.Y. in 2014. As the correctional bus pulled up to the facility, I could never have imagined beyond my wildest dreams what I'd discover up on that hill.

The prison building's structure has an intimidating appearance, with a really high wall. It's got to be at least 40 feet high. Once inside the facility, I was soon greeted by an inmate who asked me if I was interested in attending AA there. I was open to the suggestion. I had been in and out of trouble and in and out of solitary confinement. My life was pretty unmanageable.

I will always remember my first AA meeting here at Elmira. I was quite nervous. The group was called The Hill Group and it was held in the facility's school building. This one was on a Wednesday night, and I was told ahead of time that there'd be outside AA members in attendance.

I had always struggled in social settings when alcohol wasn't involved. And I was an introvert. But whatever anxiety I experienced that night subsided. I received a warm welcome by everyone at the meeting. Moreover, I had the opportunity to meet at least 20 different sober prisoners who lived in various housing units throughout the complex.

What I definitely remember is the smell of coffee brewing. The room was decorated with all these AA slogans, and there was plenty of literature—tons of it. I welcomed myself to some literature. I learned about the history of The Hill Group. It's been in existence since President Kennedy was in the White House! Also, this group has saved many, many lives of inside members, as well as outside members.

During the meeting, we went around the room reading the Preamble, the Steps and some AA literature. The chairperson that night stressed the importance of anonymity and asked if there were any newcomers, so I raised my hand. Later, we had a coffee break and when the meeting ended, we gathered and said the Lord's Prayer. They told me to come back. I'm glad I did.

At one point in my life, I wanted the world and everything in it. Unfortunately, alcohol and other substances had their way with me. I came to prison for the first time at the age of 31. I now had a sentence of 30 years to life.

I truly believe that The Hill Group has made me a better person. Prison is full of negativity and temptations. Every day above water is a good day in here. I've learned that alcoholism is a disease that strikes at random; it doesn't discriminate. When I sit in my group here and look around the room, I see guys from every conceivable walk of life. When I listen to other members share their stories, I feel something deep down inside myself. I learn that other people are no better nor less than me. We're all equal in AA regardless of how much sobriety we may or may not have.

Our elections for service at The Hill Group are coming up. I've held the literature position for the past year. It was such a rewarding experience. However, I can't say that I've read all the literature yet. I will say that what I read has made me more knowledgeable about the history of AA, how it started and why it still exists today.

Before I found AA in prison, I was labeled by the administration as a disruptive inmate. Convicts who know me can attest to that. Finding this group is saving my rear each and every day. Growing up and taking responsibility for my actions, past and present, is what I do today. It's who I am. My relationships with family and friends have improved dramatically since joining AA. Now it's about working the Steps, carrying the message and improving my relationship with my Higher Power.

I started a hobby in here about a year ago, painting subjects in different mediums. A fellow member at our group was kind enough to give me some of his extra paint brushes. This took my imagination to new levels. Recently, with help from various family members, I was able to turn my cell into a little art studio. I've painted several pieces since and sent them to family and friends for the holidays. The feedback from everyone has been overwhelming. I owe that to The Hill Group.

I've been incarcerated almost 17 years now. I may never see the outside world again. I have good days and bad ones. But don't we all? I know I must continue to change.

For me, sobriety is a gift that's earned every single day, just like most people earn a living on the outside world. Each and every hour, day, month and year that I don't pick up that first drink, I earn that gift. And then I try to help another member achieve that same reward.

Michael T.
Stormville, New York

A Good Cry at the Alcathon
June 2020

I walked into the Never Too Young meeting on the third Sunday in March. It was my fifth AA meeting and I was still struggling with the idea of being an alcoholic and never drinking again. The meeting was held in a Catholic school cafeteria with wood paneled walls and long tables. Metal folding chairs were scattered here and there. The room was packed with people chatting and laughing, coffee cups in hand, nibbling on chocolate cookies and slices of cake. I was shaky and shy and sat in the front, as suggested.

It was an anniversary meeting, the first of many I would attend. I didn't know it then but the woman celebrating 10 years of sobriety would be the woman I would ask to be my sponsor. She walked with her head held high as she approached the podium. "Hi, my name is Nicole and I'm an alcoholic," she said, smiling.

The room burst into applause. She held up a small yellow marble, a gift given to her before she left rehab. She explained, "They say that after five years you get your marbles back and after 10 years you know how to use them." Everyone laughed. It seemed to be a joke...one I didn't get, as I had just a few days sober. But I laughed anyway.

Nicole looked genuinely happy, at peace. Is that what 10 years of sobriety looked like? I wondered. I couldn't imagine someone like her ever feeling the way I felt. I couldn't imagine her being the falling-down drunk I was. And if she was, how did she look so put together now?

I had walked with my head down for so long, afraid to look anyone in the eye. But Nicole looked around the room, unafraid to be seen. She spoke with confidence and poise without any shame or guilt. She talked about being a woman of dignity, grace and gratitude. These were words I would never use to describe myself.

For the next hour, I sat and listened. And I cried. I cried because I knew that I was in the place where I needed to be. And for the first time, I saw hope of what my life could be like without drinking.

At the end of the hour, Nicole and I exchanged numbers. She was kind and encouraging. By the middle of that week, I asked her if she would be my sponsor, and because I knew Never Too Young was her home group, I made it mine too. That made four out of five suggestions to check off.

I was a 40-something single mother raising a 12-year-old son with autism and working full-time when I walked into the rooms of AA. Making 90 meetings in 90 days felt like a stretch. But they said, "meeting makers make it," so I made a meeting a day, sometimes two or three. I was grateful my home group was within walking distance.

My home group was also the first meeting where I brought my son. I had been coming around for a few weeks. I didn't see anyone bring their kids to their AA meeting and I felt awkward about it. But on a Thursday evening, I needed a meeting, and as I was without child-care, I had no choice but to bring him. I packed his computer and headphones, notebook paper and crayons. He and I sat in the back and I gave him milk and cookies.

About halfway through the meeting, my son started to get antsy and talkative. Fearing I'd be asked to leave, I gathered our things and headed out. As we got to the door, a member stopped me. "Did you get women's phone numbers?" he asked. I thanked him and said that I had.

His name was Alex. I didn't think anything of it at the time, but as the months went on, I got to know Alex. He's quiet and shy and doesn't say much. I realized that it took a lot for him to walk over and approach me. It speaks volumes about our home group and our members that he took the time to do that. The hand of AA was there for me.

As soon as I was able to take a commitment, I volunteered to make coffee. I worked as an administrative assistant for years and one of the tasks I resented most was making coffee. Something about it made me feel subservient. However, making coffee for my home group didn't bother me in the least. I was happy to do it. Making coffee seemed like a small price to pay for my sobriety.

I spent my first sober New Year's Eve at Never Too Young. They held an "alcathon," non-stop AA meetings from 7:00 A.M. to 2:00 A.M. I usually spent New Year's Eve drinking at home, alone. I'd cry into my wine until I passed out. But this was my first New Year's Eve sober and my son was going to be spending it with his dad. To say that I was scared to face the evening alone is an understatement. I needed to be in a place where I felt safe. The safest place for me was my home group, the place where I could be with friends, the people who knew me best.

Overwhelmed with emotions from grief to gratitude, I cried all New Year's Eve, moving from table to table at the alcathon with my wrinkled tissues stained with mascara crumpled in my hand. Fortunately, in between the tears, I also laughed a lot. I rang in the New Year safe and sober and surrounded by much love and fellowship.

In sobriety, I've learned to laugh through my tears. I don't feel silly crying. I'd rather cry in a meeting than home alone.

During my first year at Never Too Young, I felt more and more comfortable bringing my son. So often I've felt alone raising him. I used to be scared that I'd be kicked out of our meeting. This group embraced me and my son. During moments when fellow members see me becoming flustered or frustrated trying to quiet my son, someone will pat me on the shoulder and assure me that he's fine.

I'm always moved by the love and support of the fellowship in my home group. They remind me that I'm a good mom. They make an effort to help my son feel welcome and included. The women mother him and the men treat him like one of the guys. They understand. They're patient and extremely generous. They spoil him with milk and cookies and slices of anniversary cake. They engage with him and laugh at his sweet silliness. They greet him with hugs and high fives and always offer to help. The hand of AA reaches out. My home group reaches out. They always remind me that I am never alone.

Lisa Q.
Bronx, New York

SECTION TWO

The Joys of Service

If You Can't Live or Die, Make Coffee!
September 1988

I t has been said in these rooms that, if we all threw our problems into one pile and walked around it for a while, we'd each reach in and take back our own problems. As an active alcoholic, I wish I had a nickel for every time I found myself in that state of utter despair. God help me! What can I do? I've alienated everyone I know who means anything to me; I don't know how to behave among normal people; and I can't stop drinking! I wish I could change everything, change everyone, so things could be better. I thought I knew the answers, but for some inexplicable reason nothing seemed to work out. Everything in my life seemed to be getting progressively worse when all I wanted was to make it better. I saw that I couldn't live this way, but there seemed no other way that I could live.

Death appeared to be an alternative. If I killed myself I'd have the last say after all, and my family would benefit from the insurance. It seemed my last opportunity to write a happy ending. But I wasn't really all that macho. I was scared and I knew I was about to lose everything I'd manipulated my way into. It was as if my whole life had been meaningless. What should I do?

Make coffee! That's what some insensitive guy suggested at a meeting. "Why dwell on what you can't do? It just gets you more frustrated. Why not concentrate on what you can do and do it? You want to be of some genuine value in this world? Then come down off Mount Olympus and join us. We don't need a corporate vice president—and your other credentials don't count here. Our only concern is to help ourselves by helping each other find what we were all so desperately in search of: freedom from booze and a contented, useful life. We don't need a genius. We need a coffeemaker. You want to feel good about yourself again? Make coffee!"

They had no way of knowing what they were letting themselves in for. I'd never made a cup of coffee in my whole life, and here I was being asked to brew coffee for a crowd of people. The prospect scared me half to death, though I must admit, it took my mind off my other problems. Here was a real problem: How do I tell the group members about my fear? Well, I mustered all the courage I could and told them that I wasn't street-wise enough to make coffee. So they put two guys on it with me who knew what they were doing. Within a few weeks not only did I make a good pot of coffee (eighty cups, mind you), but I found that with the coffee maker's job came fringe benefits. They began to trust me with the key to the meeting room and it became my responsibility to set up the chairs and put out the signs for the meetings.

Thank God I didn't feel that any of this was beneath me, because as I did these things and didn't question the need for them or the reason for them (I was told it would help me stay sober), I experienced a miracle. For while I was doing these things I felt like I was a real, living, important part of this wonderful Fellowship. I belonged! It was my introduction into the now, and for the first time in years I knew serenity. I found that pushing a broom at the end of each meeting also helped me to stay sober and not because of some high-minded purpose like helping the group. No, it was more because I suspected that most, if not all, of the really sober ones had done the same thing and knew the secret of what pushing a broom can do for a big-time operator like myself. I was grateful that they loved me enough to know and give me exactly what I needed.

All I thought about as I was making the coffee was making the coffee and how people could enjoy it. At my sponsor's suggestion, I stood near the coffeepot and welcomed everyone who came by. I must have experienced a million smiles in a very short time. And when I pushed the broom all I concentrated on was the dust rising from it as I moved it across the floor. My troubles were gone for the time that I was doing these things. And so it can be for you. If you can't live and you can't die, make coffee.

Jerry B.
Freeport, New York

Unlocking the Group Conscience
February 1992

I have often heard it said that all you need to start a new AA group is a resentment and a coffeepot. Resentments had kept me drunk for many years, and in 1987 I was literally dying from alcohol and drug addiction, fueled by resentments. I sobered up at a group close to my home. The people there welcomed me and loved me and told me to keep coming back. By the grace of God, I did. These folks loved me through that first year. They hugged me and honestly shared their experience, strength, and hope. The group had broken up about a year before I came in, so we had lots of newcomers as well as just a few oldtimers, and through that first year we grew in size and I felt comfortable and at home. When my first birthday arrived they all celebrated with me. It was the best feeling I ever had. I felt loved and "a part of."

When I was sober about eighteen months, we elected a GSR from the group. Up to that point we hadn't had a GSR, and because none of us had too much time in AA we decided to allow anyone with one year of continuous sobriety to be eligible to run for the job.

I was elected. I'm sure my ego was out of control; it seemed like another popularity contest and I had won. But I decided to do my best at this position and to follow through and return to my group with a monthly report from area meetings. I fought my pride and ego before that first area meeting, and prayed for some humility. I did the best I could at the time. At the first area meeting the other GSRs welcomed me, and they talked about giving money back to central office and GSO. We didn't do that in my home group, and they told me to take it to our group conscience and to explain the need for helping on these levels. I told them we had no regular group conscience meeting and they were all amazed. We had never had elections for any positions other than GSR and alternate and a central office representative. They suggested that as GSR I call a group conscience meeting to pass on what they told me. After that meeting, I made a sign, picked a date, and posted the announcement on the board at our meeting place. The next day the sign was gone. I was told by the man who owns the building—he was a recovering alcoholic—to not put up any more signs; he said we would have no group conscience meeting unless he called one. I did try to explain what I had heard, and that as GSR it was my responsibility to pass it on. Then we argued over the telephone for a while. I said many things that day and I was in a rage by the time the conversation ended.

I cried and screamed, went to meetings, and shared my feelings. My true feelings were hurt. My ego told me I was in charge and that surely everyone would see how right I was. The man who owned the building very seldom came to meetings, so there was never any direct confrontation.

After one week of sick rage and bad feelings, no sleep and name calling, some people asked me to have the group conscience meeting anyway. I had decided before this to leave the group and find a new one, but now I decided that I was not alone, so we scheduled the group conscience on a Saturday afternoon. Once again the man called me and told me the doors would be padlocked.

At this point, I was sick and eaten up with resentment. I felt like getting drunk for the first time in a long time. On that Saturday morning, I woke up to a beautiful day that I couldn't see, and I got on my knees and prayed for courage and guidance and for God's will not mine to be done. I was scared, and I felt I had created yet another crisis, and wanted everything to be okay again. "Please God, give me what I need in order to know your will." After I got up off my knees the phone rang and it was the delegate from our state whom I had tried to contact earlier in the week. I felt calm and serene as I spoke to him.

The fear and the anger had left and I felt God's presence near me. We spoke for almost an hour, and he told me to hang in there and not to forget our primary purpose—staying sober and helping others.

We had our group conscience meeting—another group offered us their building as the doors were indeed padlocked at our meeting place. I knew I was okay when I accepted the locked doors. I didn't like it but I accepted it.

From that first group conscience meeting, a miracle happened. We now have a new group that we love and members who care about a group conscience. I pray for the man at the other group on a daily basis, and although the resentment can be refueled from time to time, I work on my part of the resentment, and feel that this was part of my spiritual growth. Our group is small but we have been there for other newcomers who need us as much as we need them. I am sober today, thank God and AA, and my Higher Power is with me, and reveals more to me each new day.

I can remember the people who loved me back to life, and I can feel content with my choices. I can't forget where I got sober, but today, I choose service, unity, and recovery. I have learned a little more of the meaning of "Live and Let Live."

Toni F.
Wichita, Kansas

Chairman of the Group
May 1974

B eing chairman of an AA group takes a lot of time and effort. Now that I am coming to the end of my term, I've been thinking a lot about this most interesting experience.

It took me a while to discover that the group really did have a conscience and an identity of its own, which had nothing to do with me. The job became a burden only when I tried to substitute my own conscience for the group's by promoting activities. I soon learned that the chairman is really a servant, an instrument.

The coffee man may seem to be the low man on the totem pole, but I considered him the key man at each meeting. So I tried to help him as much as possible. It's not an easy job, and few ever offer to help. I never left the coffee man alone, especially when it was time to clean up.

I was always early on the job, too. And every time I unlocked the door of the meeting room, I knew I was in a place I wanted to be.

I always had a few cheerful words to say to newcomers. I like new people. I need AA to stay sober, and the newcomer is the most important person if AA is to endure.

I was almost always able to be nice to cranky old-timers, who told me I was doing everything wrong.

I never gave a big buildup to a speaker I was introducing, nor did I refer to him as being a friend of mine or having been helpful to me. This is irrelevant. I let the listeners determine the speaker's worth. One man's meat may not be another's.

I never thought length of sobriety alone was enough to make a good speaker. People who have a solid dependence on AA are usually easy to listen to. I tended to avoid people who were "great on the Steps" or who had "terrific sobriety" (whatever that is). I usually did not ask a speaker who "needed to speak." I tried to ask people who were, in my estimation, good for the group.

At first, I worried a lot about speakers—whether the group would like the ones I had chosen. I worried so much, I did not enjoy the meetings. After the meetings, as I diligently swept the floor and picked up cigarette butts, I resented my poor lot. Added to this, I had to bear waves of resentment from people who felt guilty because I swept the floor. I learned to change my thinking about all of that, and I don't have those feelings any more.

The best chairman should be flexible, have a sense of humor and humility. There are few guidelines. Every group is autonomous, and what is suitable for one group may not be for another. It's not easy to keep things in reasonably good order without being bossy. It's possible for anyone to take over an AA group, and that's bad both for the group and for the person taking over—as I found out the hard way. Why does it happen? Often, because there aren't enough members interested in the work and responsibilities of group offices. I would like others to know that their participation in group activities is needed. More than that, it can be fun. A person can learn to be a good chairman—grow while serving—and that makes the job rewarding.

Anonymous
New York, New York

Group Secretary
July 1980

My copy of *Alcoholics Anonymous* suggests that if I want what you have, there are certain things that I should do—like get into action and give away what I've got, i.e., work with another alcoholic. Over and over, I hear it stated in many different ways. As our book says, the first three alcoholics in AA felt that they had to give others what they had found or be sunk. I believe you have to give it away to keep it.

Today, I am secretary of a group, and what a delight it is! Because of my course of "vigorous action," all the Promises on pages 83 and 84 are continually happening to me. I believe it is because of my involvement in AA, for the book states at the end of the Promises, "They will always materialize if we work for them." Work? I call it a pleasure, an honor, a God-given gift.

Being a secretary is a thrill. After I was five months old on the program, the group voted to elect me secretary, and right from the beginning, I liked the responsibility. I've always enjoyed meetings and the expressions of the members, "that indefinable something" in their eyes, "the stimulating and electric atmosphere," as it is described on page 160 of our Big Book.

I receive one of my greatest rewards when I announce, "If there are any newcomers," and one, two, or three stand up and give their first names. Then, after the meeting, I make myself responsible for seeing that they are invited to stick around, meet new friends, get phone numbers, and get the love and caring that I received at my first meeting. Being responsible is my way of expressing my gratefulness to God for what he has given me. When we have new friends at our meeting, I do everything I can to make them feel wanted.

Another pleasure that I receive is seeing newcomers return the following week and watching them slowly grow in the Fellowship and embrace a host of new friends who care. I once heard this definition at a meeting: "AA is people helping people." I'm proud to be a part of it.

AA has given me a purpose in life; I found it on page 77 of our Big Book: "Our real purpose is to fit ourselves to be of maximum service to God and the people about us." I cannot think of a better spot to be in to carry out that duty than being the secretary of an AA group.

Being a secretary takes me to lots of other meetings, looking for guest speakers. (There are 131 AA meetings a week in our county.) I try to take something with me from each meeting that I attend. We have a very happy alcoholic in our area by the name of Maria. Members often ask her how they can get some of that happiness. She asks, "How do you want to be? If you want to be happy, go to a meeting. If you want to be twice as happy, go to two meetings. And if you want to be *really* happy, like me, go to lots and lots of meetings!"

I stick close to my friend Linda at meetings. I always like what she says. Once, I overheard a conversation with Linda and a newcomer that went like this: "But Linda, I don't believe in God. And people tell me—"

"That's okay. Just don't drink, and go to meetings!" I've been following hints like this for eight and a half years, and they work.

In Denver in 1975 at the International Convention, I heard many great things, but one that stands out is: "The key to happiness is not to concentrate on yourself, but to lose yourself in others." I liked what Carl W. told our group when he ended his talk with these words for the new people: "Let us love you until you can learn to love yourselves." When I was new in AA, I heard, "If you can't use it right now, put it on a shelf for later." Today, I find myself reaching for many of these gems. Someone asked Jim C. if the Big Book would show him how to get sober. Jim replied, "No. But it will teach you how to stay sober!"

I visit our central office often to pick up literature and books, and I'm reminded of the time I went to a meeting out of town and brought back a bunch of little booklets of knowledge, poems, and prayers. Trying to do something extra for my group, I placed one on each chair, then I opened the meeting with a prayer that I read out of one booklet. After the meeting was over, an older member came up to me with one of the little folders and asked if it was AA literature. I said, "Uh, no. I guess not." Then he explained that it was too deep and too complicated. He further explained that our own literature is reviewed by AA committees. From that day on, I have made sure that the books and literature are those approved by the AA General Service Conference.

At every meeting, I ask for volunteers to answer calls for help from the still-suffering alcoholic. We have an ample supply of Twelfth Step forms to be filled out and returned to the central office.

For me, the way I achieve happiness is to start each day with love in my life and give it to others. I try to follow the directions on page 86 of the Big Book. I ask my Higher Power daily to direct my thinking and give me inspiration—and so much good stuff comes my way that I *have* to give it away.

H. R.
Millbrae, California

The Sponsor Broker
September 2004

The Loyola Men's Group of Portland, Oregon has been in existence for over forty-five years, and we have a very strong tradition of reaching out to newcomers. The group moved to a new, larger location in the middle of 1998. During the following months, our attendance doubled in size to about 150 per week. We had so many new alcoholics arriving that we needed to develop better ways to welcome the new people and invite them to be a part of our group. So we took a good look at ourselves during a two-month group inventory in early 1999. Invigorated by that process, we developed a number of ways to improve the quality of our home group— for everyone, not just for the newcomers.

Loyola Greeter Teams are groups of five or six men who reach out to newcomers before and after our weekly meeting. They give out informational welcome packets and their personal phone numbers. They also ask the newcomers for their phone numbers in order to allow follow-up calls. The Greeters are asked to stand up during the announcements at the middle of the meeting so they are visible to everyone, and then they make themselves available for at least twenty minutes after the meeting as well. We have found that old-timers are really energized when they take their turn as Greeters. And, better yet, more of the newcomers are coming back week after week.

Phone Trees are groups of three alcoholics who commit to visiting with each other by telephone, or meeting face-to-face at least once a week, outside of the meeting. The Trees are rotated every three months from a list of voluntary participants, and newcomers are always mixed in with old-timers. The continually expanding communication among group members has been remarkable since we established our Phone Trees. "One alcoholic talking to another" is the foundation of the entire AA Fellowship, and it definitely works in our home group.

We've also created a better way to encourage sponsorship. Like many groups, we ask newcomers to introduce themselves at the beginning of the meeting. In the past, we'd suggest that they get a sponsor, but we did very little to help them with this suggestion. As a result, many of the newcomers drifted away without ever making a good connection with a sponsor. The simple truth is that many newcomers find it very difficult to reach out to complete strangers. Compounding this problem, many old-timers are distracted by their own busy lives and their established friendships. One night last year, all that changed for us at Loyola. A long-time member of the group stood up during the announcements and said, "If you want a sponsor, talk to me after the meeting. I'll hook you up with someone." That was the night the Sponsor Broker was created.

It took our new Sponsor Broker about six months of flying blind to sort out an efficient and effective way to get all these different alcoholics connected with each other. On virtually every night since that announcement, our Sponsor Broker has had new people requesting his services after the meeting. He emphasizes that his job is to make a match for temporary sponsorship. It is always up to the individuals to decide if they want to keep working with each other. During the past year, he has put together more than ninety pairs of alcoholics, and well over thirty have evolved into full-time relationships.

The first task for the Sponsor Broker is to create a list of willing sponsors. The list was developed by recruiting old-timers, talking with other members for suggestions, and making general announcements at the meeting. We have learned that an effective Sponsor Broker needs to be an outgoing, active member of the group. This is not a job for wallflowers.

The next step is to collect some information from potential sponsors and sponsees. We ask for name, address, and phone number so that people can contact each other. We request information about the individual's age, AA history, and treatment history, as well as marital and parental experience—all of which helps the Sponsor Broker make an effective match. We believe it's important that men volunteering to be sponsors have their own sponsor. (In fact, quite a few old-timers who had drifted away from their original sponsors now have new sponsors thanks to the efforts of our Sponsor Broker.) We have also learned that the most productive relationships seem to develop between people who regularly attend the same home group.

Experience has shown that the best time to make a match is right at the meeting. When a new man reaches out, we are ready for him, and can suggest a sponsor who can begin working with the newcomer that night. The Sponsor Broker must be willing to tell people what to do to get things rolling. If the first match is not working for whatever reason, the Sponsor Broker is always willing to make another match to get the new man connected.

We have found that the key ingredient for success at the beginning of these new relationships between sponsor and sponsee is the followup by the sponsor. If long-time AA members take some of the initiative during those first few weeks, newcomers seem to come back more frequently and get active in the group more quickly. The 500-pound telephone that we have all experienced applies only to out-going calls—incoming calls are light as a feather! When we reach out to a newcomer with a few phone calls, we are teaching by example that reaching out is the way to stay connected and stay sober.

While recruiting potential sponsors, we have discovered that many long-time members of AA do not feel confident in their ability to sponsor other alcoholics. In addition, some members are uncertain about the time commitment involved with sponsorship, while a few others are just plain lazy. Our Sponsor Broker has developed his own gentle and not-so-gentle ways to encourage and guide people past their own reluctance to become sponsors. Some alcoholics actually need a little education, while others just need a shove in the right direction. Like so many things in our Fellowship, the amazing benefits of sponsorship cannot be fully understood until they are experienced.

Sponsorship education has become an ongoing process for our group. We have an audiotape available of a sponsorship workshop given by one of our long-time members at a local convention. Another reliable source of information is a pamphlet from AA World Services, Inc. called "Questions & Answers on Sponsorship." Recently, we have conducted a series of one-hour sponsorship seminars which have been held before the first meeting of the month. The seminars consist of a dozen or so group members each speaking for three to four minutes on their specifically assigned topic concerning sponsorship. Some of the topics from the past four months include: making a place for yourself in AA; start with the First Step; using the phone; daily maintenance; switching addictions; keeping secrets; recovery on the road; slips; thirteenth-stepping; understanding God; and sponsors don't need to know all the answers. These monthly seminars have significantly energized our group and have taught us much about sponsorship. We have also shared the audiotapes of these seminars with other AA members in our area.

The Sponsor Broker has become a truly valuable service position at the Loyola Men's Group. Our group has become more vibrant since that night when one man stood up and said, "If you want a sponsor, talk to me after the meeting. I'll hook you up with someone." Long-time members are more involved in the group, reaching out to newcomers and becoming more active with their own sponsors. We see more new people coming to our meetings, getting connected, and staying sober. Our group is more fully experiencing what the Big Book describes on page 89: "Life will take on new meaning. To watch people recover, to see them help others, to watch loneliness vanish, to see a fellowship grow up about you, to have a host of friends—this is an experience you must not miss. We know you will not want to miss it. Frequent contact with newcomers and with each other is the bright spot of our lives."

Brian F.
Portland, Oregon

Getting the Red Out
April 1982

I collided with the AA Traditions when I was five months dry. The social dropouts in the Lower Manhattan neighborhood group whose meetings I graced with my presence twice a week, only because I would die if I didn't, elected me group treasurer.

I admired their judgment. I was brighter than ever with each drinkless day and clearly superior to anyone clearly inferior. *Noblesse oblige*, so I obliged them.

They didn't tell me then that nobody else had wanted the job.

They didn't tell me their Second Tradition meant they could ignore what I said if they didn't agree with it.

They never even mentioned the nub of their Seventh Tradition, which I've come to call "the treasurer's own." Alcoholics and money don't mix well, they could have warned me then. But at that time, I would simply have thought they were apologizing for the sorry state of their books.

They gave me an antique brown accordion envelope wadded with old receipts, and $53 to put in it, their total worth. A red and black dime-store, double-entry ledger, kept as if by a scribbling chicken, showed wild swings from gain to loss over four years and a current alltime low. Cash flow was negative. Income was off. Spending was lavish on coffee, sugar, milk, cookies, and cups. But one single, gross expense outpaced them all: At the end of each month, almost without fail, in an evident excess of misguided charity, a prodigal sum was squandered on cake, no less, for a member named "Anny."

This group needed smart management! I would cut expenses immediately, leaving "Anny," whoever she was, to the end of the month when she came to claim her cake. I would take her aside then and explain (gently) that she would have to leave if she counted on us for anything more than sobriety.

Back in the kitchen, I set rules: one less quart of milk, one less box of cookies per meeting. Name-brand coffee was out; house labels were in. Cups could be had in quantity at bargain prices if one knew where to shop.

Expenses dropped. The idea of quantity discounts so impressed the group's grocery buyers that one brought in a cut-rate case of sixty-watt bulbs that he proceeded to sell to members at cost. By the end of the meeting, he was sold out.

After each meeting, I walked home alone, jangling with change, drunk on power. Neatly, I entered income and expenses for the evening in my scuffed ledger and then, exhilarated by my mind's new ability to retain consecutive thoughts, sat into the night to juggle figures on a desk calculator and draw up projections for the group's future success. But the reports I prepared for the other officers kept coming back to me, apparently unread. Were they sending me a message? I knew they weren't getting mine. I had advanced a plan to tap a so-far-untouched source of revenue: beginners' meetings. Beginners ate too many cookies, drank too much coffee, and were never asked to pay a penny. Passing them the basket seemed only fair. I decided to take it up personally with a member I had begun to trust. He suggested coffee after the meeting, and I accepted. I had never done that before.

"You know," he said, "anytime I see an AA member climbing the walls about money, I see a person in real trouble." He had misunderstood or, worse, hadn't been listening. So I told him again that without money from the beginners, the group itself was in real trouble; we would never get out of the red. He agreed to discuss it with the leaders.

The basket appeared at beginners' meetings, on the speaker's table. It was never mentioned and never passed, and it never snared a cent. Yes, they were sending me a message, but I wasn't getting it. These people stomped on solvency. Maybe they couldn't handle money, or shrank from its potential. They wouldn't know what to do with a surplus if they had it.

By my seventh month in charge, in fact, we did have a modest reserve fund. I decided to find out what they might want to do with it. I had in mind a savings account.

I called for a business meeting. I accounted for my stewardship, then presented my plan: A little nest egg tucked away not only would constrain us to live within our current means, but would mean investment in the future, expanding of itself by five and a half percent even as we watched. Who knew where it could lead us?

One of the food buyers raised his hand. "Maybe that's a good idea. We could save up for a party."

The boss of all bosses always sat in the back. He spoke up. To me. "How much money do you have now?"

How often would I have to explain this? I told him again it was $120. "How much do you pay in rent each month?"

"Fifty."

"What do you send every month to AA services?"

"Right now I'm sending ten dollars apiece to Intergroup, the Institutions Committee, and GSO."

He rose thoughtfully. "Nobody in this group . . ." He struck deeper. "*Nobody* in this group has any business stashing money. What do you think this is—some kind of a bank? We carry the message, and that's it. We keep what's important by giving it away, and nobody here can afford to forget that! How much were you planning to put in this savings account of yours?"

I had started to shake inside. "I guess about thirty," I got out. I had planned on forty.

"I move we take your thirty dollars and send it to GSO, Intergroup, and Institutions. Cut it any way you like. And from here on in, let's up our contributions to them all by five dollars apiece." He sat down.

He was trying to wipe me out! They all were! They were voting. All their hands were up! So I raised mine, too.

I was out the door before the chairman could report the vote. I knew what I had to do. I carried out their instructions to the letter, then stayed away.

Finally, I did go back, and there was the cake for "Anny," and I was one of the month's anniversary celebrants. I pinned the corsage they gave me to the red wool dress I hadn't worn in six years, because I'd been too fat. "Believe it or not," I heard myself saying from the front of the room, "I am a member of this group," and they applauded.

A year later, I was chairman of another group. I had a bright idea: "Let's have the beginners take up the collection, so they can feel more at home with the group."

The man who handled the baskets got the jitters. "How can we trust the beginners not to take some of the money for themselves?"

"Listen," I told him, "you can't get uptight about money, or you're in real trouble. We'll just have to trust them. The money is incidental."

I smiled inside when I heard that. I was in the black at last.

C. D.
Washington, D.C.

AA in Cyberspace: Online and Active
May 2003

For sixteen years, I was an active member of AA, doing all the usual stuff: going to several meetings a week, sponsoring people, enjoying service work in many different capacities, and meeting with AA friends throughout the week. I have always loved meetings (they have never been a "must" for me), and have been blessed with a host of dear friends in the Fellowship, including my husband whom I met in AA. Together our spiritual and social lives are centered in Alcoholics Anonymous.

Then, a little over four years ago, with no discernible warning, I was struck by several severe illnesses and struck hard. I suddenly entered into what has been, up to now, the most difficult period of my entire life. I became so critically ill that I was barely able to eat or drink, let alone attend AA meetings. I came very close to death. This is not how I had envisioned my early forties, or any time of my life, for that matter. Yet, as always, life must be lived on life's terms. Suddenly, I was unable to do hundreds of things that I had done before. The losses were, and are, beyond description. And do you know what I missed the most of all? Fellowship. My meetings. I felt so sad every time another meeting passed at my home group without me there. I was struggling to survive, and I needed the sustenance of my AA friends and seeing the program at work in their lives. I needed the reminders that "I am not alone," that with HP we can walk through whatever comes our way, and all the other great blessings that fellowship brings into our lives.

At first, my husband and I hoped that this would be a short illness, but that has not been the case. After seven months without a meeting, I was desperate. I got on the phone, and the outcome was that a small group of women began to come to my home once a week. These women brought hope and love to me for two years, and we all benefited from our meeting, until each of our lives changed and that meeting had to come to an end.

Fortunately, in the meantime, I had put aside my "contempt prior to investigation" and obtained access to the Internet and joined two online email meetings. This was a scary step for me, because I was afraid of the Internet and dubious about online meetings. But I knew it was important for me to try.

Now, I have been blessed by the joy and fellowship of Alcoholics Anonymous once again and in a new way. This May I will have been sober twenty years, the last four of which have been maintained solely by online fellowship (and literature, including Grapevine). Contrary to my fears, I have found very good sobriety online. I have done a more serious and in-depth study of the Big Book than I ever did in face-to-face book studies. I have made several close friends before and after the meetings, and we have cherished and enriching friendships, despite the physical distance between our homes.

Although most of my AA friends have been supportive of me, I have also heard small rumblings of criticism about online AA and how it is harming or threatening to harm our great Fellowship. I beg to differ. Quite honestly, if I could go to my home group tonight, I would be there. I would so love to get the hugs and smiles and tears in person that I can only read about online. But that does not mean that my online meetings are "less than" or "not real AA" or any of the other criticisms that are, I believe, based in fear. I cherish these online meetings just as dearly as the face-to-face meetings I wish I could attend.

I believe that if there are people avoiding face-to-face meetings and "hiding out" online, they are not the kind of people who are active online either. They would not suddenly overcome their shyness, resentment, or fear, and show up at face-to-face meetings if they were forced to by having no online AA to go to. The people I know who are active in my email meetings are people who always have chosen to be active in AA. They are, like me, ill and very grateful to have meetings they can still attend on the Internet, or they are people who are active both online and at face-to-face meetings (as I hope to be someday).

In the meantime, I have found plenty of opportunities for service in Alcoholics Anonymous online: there is no shortage of newcomers and not-so-newcomers needing support and love; there are always jobs that need doing. The Twelfth Step is being worked in a myriad of ways among us, along with the other Steps, Traditions, and Concepts of our program.

My Higher Power has once again given me the tools I need to stay sober and to live as comfortably as I can with unresolved difficulties. If possible, my sobriety has grown even deeper and more meaningful to me during the last four years, partly because of my experiences, which have drawn me very close on a daily basis to my HP and taught me a lot about present-moment living, acceptance, compassion, and patience. Definitely, my life has been enhanced by the sharing and fellowship I find here on my computer, twenty-four hours a day, seven days a week.

Please do not be afraid of online Alcoholics Anonymous. As in meetings everywhere, there are positive and negative folks, newcomers and old-timers, wisdom to be shared, and friends to be made online. Alcoholics Anonymous is alive and well on the Internet; as usual, it's all a matter of perception. Looking through the lens of deep gratitude, I see a new medium that has given me the opportunity to be an active and vital member of this great family of Alcoholics Anonymous, a family that has saved my life and continues to enhance it daily.

Kris M.
Chino, California

Big Books & Cheesecake
November 2015

My home group is the Serenity Corner Group in District 2, Area 82. We meet every Thursday evening at 8 P.M. We're in the meeting list for this district, so if you're ever up this way and in need of a meeting, please come visit. We study the 12 Steps and the 12 Traditions. At our business meetings, we explore the 12 Concepts. We like to eat delicious things, so there's always cheesecake, pie, or cookies at our regular meetings; and when we have a business meeting, we kick it off with a potluck supper. We believe in fellowship, there's no doubt about that. We enjoy the meetings before the meeting and the meetings after the meeting, almost as much as we enjoy the meeting we planned on having.

We're big on sponsorship here. Almost everyone who attends our group is sponsored by one of us. I'm always overcome by gratitude when I watch one of the guys I sponsor giving his number to a newcomer.

I have extra time on my hands these days. I suppose I could spend it doing yard work, or playing golf, or sitting around the coffee shop swapping war stories with other guys my age, but that isn't what I choose to do. Every Saturday afternoon, one or two of the new guys (or gals) at our meeting will come over and spend the day with my wife and me. Nancy and I usually put together some kind of meal, a barbecue if the weather is nice. I make cheesecake. Sometimes the newcomers bring food, or they help us make supper. It makes them feel a part of, instead of apart from.

The rest of the afternoon we devote to Step work. We read the Big Book. Slowly. Often, we pause and relate experiences we've had to something we've read. We enjoy passing it on. Ironically, we often learn more from these discussions than the newcomers do.

Let me tell you something one of them said. He was in a meeting during his first week and he felt that he didn't belong there because he was so much younger than everyone else. I had mentioned to him that we should go to a particular meeting because one of its members was celebrating 50 years of sobriety. My newcomer friend did the math in his head and figured that, if this fellow had been sober all those years, he must have started when he was young, probably in his mid-20s, about the same age as my newcomer friend. Now, my friend doesn't think he's so young.

The way my newcomer friend looks at things is changing. About a month ago, it was our group's turn to take our meeting to the local detox. Because our group is service-oriented, we encourage the new people to help us with this. One of the new women, four months sober I think, was worried that she might have to talk at the meeting. I said, "Don't worry; I'll be the one there with the longest period of sobriety. I'll speak." She breathed a sigh of relief and agreed to come to help us set up the meeting. After the meeting got underway, I asked the newcomers from our meeting to share first. OK, so I fibbed, but what a powerful meeting it was. I was amazed to watch this handful of recently sober men and women telling another group of beginners how grateful they were for the opportunity to come there to pass along their experience, strength and hope. I was even more amazed when I saw the glimmers of hope in the eyes of the alcoholics in the detox as they realized that perhaps someday soon, they might be able to do that too.

Bernie S.
Dartmouth, Nova Scotia

My 6:45 AM Family
April 2018

My alarm goes off at 6 A.M. and I roll out of bed. Every morning of the workweek I say I'm not going to the meeting, but the truth is, I don't know a better way to start my day. I roll into my home group at 6:45 A.M., searching for some java with eyes barely open. I need to get my mind right before the day begins. I also like the coffee. We all bring our own mugs. My sponsor gave me mine. It made me feel a part of the meeting and cared about. I bet she didn't know when she gave me that mug how much it meant to me to be included and welcomed into the group like that.

When I walk into the room, I feel the love. As a newcomer, I was overwhelmed. These people were serious. There was a Big Book study, a Twelve and Twelve table, a Step-Taking group, a Promise table. They had a meditation meeting twice a week. It was a one-stop AA shop. And we believe in making the newcomer feel welcome. For us, sobriety ranges from a few days to 30 years and everything in between.

Maybe it's the early morning twilight that keeps us open. It's the beginning of the day so defenses aren't up, perhaps. Whatever the reason, the honesty in that meeting humbles my soul. I have been estranged from my family for a long time and accepted the void that left. The people at this meeting have become my family. They have been there for me in good times and bad, inside that meeting and out. We continue to live life together, on life's terms. I hear over and over again that it's the fellowship that helps keep us sober. We never have to feel alone again unless we choose to.

If you need a ride to the meeting, Doug will pick you up. If you have a court date to go to, Beth is there with her calm presence. Peggy makes most situations funny, just in case you're feeling too serious. If you want to take the Step Study, Mary Beth will walk you through it. If you are looking for honesty, Leanne will keep it real. Ben will sit down and talk with the newcomer. Mike hits up the meetings at recovery centers to share hope. Boston Dave will tell you how he tried to dissect the Big Book to solve sobriety. They will all gladly tell you their hope, along with what worked and what didn't work for them.

The vast majority of the people at my home group are sponsors and give back on a regular basis. They are my heroes and I wake up in the morning hoping to follow in their footsteps. They have inspired me to work the Steps and give it away. I couldn't think of a better place to call home.

Bena P.
Madison Heights, Michigan

SECTION THREE

The Lessons of Experience

Will We Squander Our Inheritance?
June 1978

Bill W. wrote to Dr. Bob in 1949: "The groups will eventually take over, and maybe they will squander their inheritance when they get it. It is probable, however, that they won't. Anyhow, they really have grown up; AA is theirs; let's give it to them."

As a sober member of AA for more than twenty-seven years, I see some disturbing differences between what I was taught in the beginning and what is happening now. What has happened to the pride we AAs have traditionally taken in saying, "I belong to the Guttersnipe Group"? To our feeling that each one of us takes part in the group's primary purpose—carrying the message? I see groups that regularly have thirty people at meetings, but only five active members. Who takes responsibility for the necessary jobs—group offices, sponsorship, coffee making? Is the AA group dying because of individual apathy?

The Responsibility Declaration is basic to AA thinking: "I am responsible. When anyone, anywhere, reaches out for help, I want the hand of AA always to be there. And for that: I am responsible." Yet central offices seem to be having more and more difficulty finding sober AAs to make Twelfth Step calls. One of the first things I learned is that I need the newcomer as much as he needs me, yet some members feel they are doing new people a favor by getting in touch with them. Are we trying to hold on to sobriety now by not giving it away?

I wonder how many are lost because we don't have the time—or won't make the time—to share or care. What about the still-suffering drunk who calls AA and is told where the meeting is—and to go by himself? What of the newcomer who goes to a meeting and finds no one to talk to? Or is told to call other members but is given no names or numbers? When I was called on by an AA member, I joined a group and got a sponsor. The group gave me a list of members, with addresses and phone numbers, to use when needed. Today, there seems to be little follow-up, little caring, few phone calls.

How many alcoholics have we lost simply because they were never really accepted? Do sober members still say, "Hey, how are you doing? Call me if you get shook up, no matter what time it is. Remember, we need you"? Alcoholics may be getting sober, not because of us, but in spite of us.

I have talked to many older members who feel as I do. Remember, AA is not going to preserve itself automatically. What are we, each one of us, doing with the gift of sobriety, so freely and lovingly given? Will we soon squander our magnificent inheritance?

Perhaps each one of us should hold on to these thoughts: "Keep me mindful of the responsibilities that accompany the blessings of freedom. The only time that wrong can prevail is when good people do nothing."

G. G.
Phoenix, Arizona

The Rise and Fall of a Home Group
October 1987

Once upon a time there was a home group of Alcoholics Anonymous. I say "once upon a time," because this group no longer exists. It folded one day after many, many years of serving the alcoholics in its community. Why?

I found this meeting to be a very healthy group of Alcoholics Anonymous. There were many old-timers to be seen talking with new people, there were greeters at the door, a secretary, treasurer, and a GSR all discussing group business. New people were welcomed with a cup of coffee and a handshake. The group just beamed with happy people. A large crowd each week caused many tables to be filled and seats were hard to come by. The last Tuesday of each month the group broke down into smaller groups for table discussion meetings. The rest of the meetings each week were closed speaker/discussion meetings and again seats were hard to come by and getting there early was common knowledge. Coffee was always ready for the first early person to arrive and there was always fellowship after the meeting. Sound good? Maybe this is *your* home group?

One meeting, after a group conscience discussion, a woman was offered the responsibility of GSR. She got the job after discussion about whether she would be good for the group. She started attending area assemblies and GSR workshops to learn about the Traditions and how they helped groups stick to their primary purpose. She learned about Conference-approved literature and how it shouldn't be mixed in with other literature to confuse the new people about which is AA's and which is not. She also learned about money in the Fellowship, the 60-3010 and other plans, and not using basket money to buy outside literature. This was exciting to me to watch this group becoming informed on issues that affected it as one group within the larger AA.

But then, slowly, the group's customs and practices began to erode. At one group business meeting the GSR pointed out that the literature the group literature representative had purchased was not Conference-approved literature and was purchased with money intended for AA use. This business meeting ended with the literature representative throwing the outside literature order forms at the group and leaving.

Later at another business meeting, discussion was held on whether an interpreter for the hearing impaired could be allowed to attend a closed meeting. The group conscience decided against it, since it was a closed meeting. An old-timer, in disagreement, took the matter before the people attending that night's meeting whether they were members of that group or not. The people attending voted to reverse the decision of the group conscience by opening the meeting to anyone. That meeting conscience weakened the effectiveness of that *group* conscience, and more people left the group.

This group was so well-attended the church adjusted the rent accordingly. But money was always there because of the number of people who attended the meetings. The group became so effective in carrying the message that a local alcoholism referral agency began sending its new young people to the Tuesday meeting as an introduction to AA. This drew other young people to the meeting and eventually it began to be known as a great place for young people to meet. Within a year after this flood of young people, a local center for troubled children began sending some of its clients to the meeting also. By this time some of the old-timers had found other Tuesday meetings to attend. When asked why, they said, "We are not hearing the language of AA that we need to hear to stay sober." Others thought the real reasons might be age differences, dress, language of the street, and just plain being outnumbered young to old.

A powerful principle in AA, rotation—the passing-it-on to the newer people—was needed in order for the group to grow. This time there was no discussion by group conscience about who would be best for the group or who was sober, but rather anyone who would volunteer got the responsibilities. Secretary, treasurer, and GSR were passed on to people who didn't know the first thing about the principles of AA or anything of the Traditions in action. Once a chairman offered the Traditions for a discussion topic one night and they were turned into feelings, drug talk, Freudian concepts, and rehab language. He never came back and neither did the former officers of the group. The group had become a group of the blind leading the blind.

Group conscience began discussing the topics: how do we get older people to return, how are we going to pay this high rent? What are we going to do?

A local DCM was asked to attend a group conscience meeting to listen and offer some suggestions. They talked about the Traditions, Steps, outside literature, getting sober people to chair the meetings, turning radios off, and the quality of sobriety that action in AA offers. A plea went out to older members to please return to the meeting. A few did return, but for only a short time. These kids seemed to be left on their own. A new group conscience emerged, struggled for a short time, and failed again when volunteers were needed to fill the frequently vacated group responsibilities. Again, there was no leadership from the now "younger old-timers," as they too left for other groups. Finally, with the rent too much, no coffee, no unity, our home group met last week to announce the end.

Bill W. said that the force which will destroy Alcoholics Anonymous will come very slowly from inside the Fellowship. This group lasted some fourteen to seventeen years. AA consists of home groups, and as a Fellowship we are seeing a breakdown of this principal structure.

If we as a Fellowship don't carefully pass on to newer members the responsibilities that come with being a group, many more groups will go the way of this group. The old-timers must stick around to teach the newer members "how it works," not only in the Twelve Steps but in our groups. Sometimes the new people must drag the answers out of the old-timers, and if they are not at the meetings, we will repeat the mistakes made early in the Fellowship.

We must learn how to keep this Fellowship alive and our groups intact for the next member who needs it. By helping insure the sobriety of others to come, we insure our own sobriety today. The best member of Alcoholics Anonymous that one can be is the best member of a home group that one can be.

W. S.
Rochester, New York

Keeping the Meeting Alive
July 1991

At a recent meeting of our home group on the First Tradition, it was suggested that one of the ways we could actively promote the principle of unity was to draft a letter sharing our recent experiences with readers of Grapevine.

About three years ago, two people sat down in a church at a meeting where attendance had dwindled down to just the pair of them and an occasional third or fourth. The meeting—though established many years previously and having been quite well-attended during several periods—was dying. The two discussed abandoning the meeting. It was several months behind on its small rent, and the weekly attendance didn't give much hope for survival.

A group conscience of the two was held; the two people decided they would fight to keep the meeting alive, that they would show up every week no matter what, and that (since they had little else to do) they would study the Big Book. The format was simple: Read a couple of paragraphs, then comment on what was read.

A strange thing happened. The few people who did show up started to come back—every week. The small group grew slowly and developed a personality. There was a lot of laughter, warm-hearted friendliness, and a sense of unity in our common goal of survival. Under the levity was a profound seriousness when it came to studying the Big Book and reaching out to newcomers.

The potent combination of fun and recovery straight from the Big Book soon paid off and within a few months attendance was close to a dozen. After the first year, the group had grown to over twenty regular attendees. We were blessed with van-loads of people from various treatment centers, so there was ample opportunity for the experienced members of the now-established group to reach out, and soon we were all busy sponsoring people through the Steps and watching the sixty-day, six-month, and one-year chips get passed out with a regularity that brought tears to our eyes and the "age of miracles" to our doorstep.

After the first year, we were nearly caught up on back rent; after the second, we were voluntarily raising our own rent and paying it quarterly in advance. Our contributions to central office, area, and general services grew and will likely remain substantial.

The group became a magnet for Big Book "thumpers" and soon we felt the need to expand to another night during the week. Six of the more active members met at a roundup to discuss it and, after securing a location, we began a second meeting, which also took its topic from the Big Book. It is based strongly on the Fifth Tradition. With our rapidly growing numbers and powerful desire to carry the message, we also started a women's meeting and began hosting a meeting with a recovery center.

We elected officers in compliance with the suggestions of the pamphlet "The A.A. Group," and they actually attend their respective meetings and report back to the group. We call ourselves Fifth Traditionists and constantly remind ourselves and each other that the reason we are here is to help the new person find what we have discovered through the Steps—not to glorify ourselves, not to discuss at nauseating length our own opinions or feelings, but to give to others what has been given to us.

Chairpeople rotate so that no one person influences a meeting for too long. Anniversaries are regular and much celebrated occurrences. There is a great sense of purpose and satisfaction among us. If we could say one thing above all else, it would be that when we followed the directions given in the book *exactly*, the newcomer recovered; when we followed the Traditions *exactly*, the group flourished.

It took some of us a very long time to discover these simple truths. But our AA experience is now so fulfilling, so positive, so full of harmonious action, we hope we never forget them.

Kathryn K.
Phoenix, Arizona

That Old Sinking Feeling
March 1990

I guess all alcoholics are familiar with it: that sudden sinking feeling in the pit of the stomach, a sense of apprehension, an inner voice of impending doom.

A lot of things can trigger it. A phone ringing in the middle of the night. A letter from the IRS.

The flashing red lights of a police car appearing suddenly in your rear-view mirror.

But since I put the cork back in the bottle, a moment of rational thought generally replaces the unreasoning fear. The phone call turns out to be a wrong number, the letter from the IRS is a routine notice, and the police car speeds by on some other errand. Besides, I have little to fear these days. My financial affairs are in honest, if not good, shape. Were I to get pulled over for exceeding the speed limit by a mile or two, I wouldn't have to worry about my breath.

The other day, however, something out of the ordinary happened and that old sinking feeling momentarily came back. I've been thinking about it ever since.

I had arrived for one of my regular meetings, a noontime one, and after parking my car I walked briskly to the side of the church where it is held. I was feeling better already because just the anticipation of a cup of coffee with AA friends followed by an hour of sharing is enough to brighten up the rest of my day.

I put my hand on the door knob and pulled. The door didn't give. I was sure it opened out but since I probably haven't cleared up completely, I tried pushing. Nothing. So I pulled again. It was locked. I rattled it, banged on it, but nobody came and I started to act with the old emotional knee-jerk reactions of panic.

Did I have the wrong day? Was my watch wrong? Had the group moved? Was there some reason for no meeting today? Maybe the church needed the room? Why hadn't they announced it? Why hadn't somebody at least put a notice on the door?

Then I realized there was, indeed, something on the door: the familiar AA sign proclaiming that there was a meeting today. Reason returned. Obviously the door had somehow been accidentally locked behind the last person to enter.

And so I went around to one of the basement windows. I could see people inside, drinking their coffee, talking, and laughing. I rapped on the glass and someone looked up and waved, wondering why I was peering in like a peeping Tom. Once they understood my plight they went around and opened the door.

Everybody, of course, had a good laugh. During the discussion meeting that followed, several people good-naturedly expressed the hope that being locked out hadn't given me a resentment. As I said, however, I've been thinking about it since.

What if the doors to AA could really be locked against me? What if it was possible to take away my membership? Maybe because I hadn't paid my dues, or because I didn't meet some ethical or ethnic standards, or maybe because I "broke the rules" by going out and getting drunk, as I have a few times during my long association with the Fellowship?

But then I recall the Preamble, and the Third Tradition, those words I so often hear without really listening, like the Lord's Prayer or the Pledge of Allegiance.

"The only requirement for A.A. membership," it says, "is a desire to stop drinking."

Since I meet that requirement, the doors of AA will always be opened to me. I need never be on the outside looking in through a basement window at the happy faces within.

And thank God—and Bob and Bill and everyone who makes the coffee and opens the meeting rooms and hangs the AA signs on the door—for that. Because without AA I know the only other antidote for those fears, imagined and real, would be the anesthesia that comes in a bottle. And that's what brought me to AA on my knees in the first place.

Ed F.
Park Ridge, New Jersey

St. Paul's Four Discussion Groups
December 1945

The present plan of discussions for new members in the St. Paul Group, with modifications during use, has been in operation for seven months. In general, the plan is to cover the AA program as clearly, concisely, and completely as possible in four 45 minute discussions, with time for questions at the end of each. New members are urged to attend all of the sessions in the proper order. At every meeting the three objectives of AA are kept before the group:

1. To attain and maintain the fact of sobriety.
2. To recover from those things that caused us to drink.
3. To help others who want what we have.

Attendance at discussions indicates the accomplishment of the fact of sobriety, so that emphasis is placed on a program of recovery. Each of the Twelve Steps is considered in respect to its place in the whole program rather than for its value per se.

Questions are encouraged at the end of the discussions and frequently require as much time as the discussion. Older members also are urged to attend discussions and many do attend. Their contributions in the question period are very valuable.

Discussion No. I—The Admissions:

1. The admission of alcoholism, as a result of our experiences with it—what we are and how we got that way.
2. The admission that we want to do something about it—the qualification for AA membership.
3. The belief that we can obtain help—which is not debatable.

A brief outline of the purpose and scope of the discussions is stated. A brief history of AA and a statement of the motives, methods and scope is made. A short consideration of what constitutes an alcoholic and a statement of alcoholism as a disease, along with the progress in public thinking about alcoholics and alcoholism, are included. The objectives in AA membership are pointed out and certain mechanisms for getting over the tough spots are mentioned.

At the end, each new member is given a small card. On one side of this card is a list of the activities at the club rooms for each night in the week, with the address of the club rooms. At the top is a reminder— "I Made a 24-Hour Deal Today," at the bottom — "Easy Does It." On the reverse side of the card is an outline of the program of recovery, which is also the outline of the discussions. Space is provided for the name and telephone number of the sponsor and co-sponsor. The new member is also given a single sheet of information about the St. Paul Group and other brief information which may be of value to him.

Discussion No. II—Inventory and Restitution:
The Steps concerned with inventory are read and discussed with regard to what constitutes an inventory, how to go about it and when to do it. Emphasis is on honesty, thoroughness, clear thinking and "follow through" in practicing the Tenth Step. Restitution is approached in the same fashion and the Steps concerned are discussed as means to an end. The Fifth Step is mentioned as a further aid in self-understanding and as a way to do something about our character analysis.

Discussions No. III & IV—Spiritual Aspects of the Program:
Steps Two, Three, Five, Seven, and Eleven are read and discussed in their relation to our objectives to the remainder of the program. Openmindedness, tolerance, and personal understanding of a higher power are stressed as essential to progress in this part of the program. "Easy Does It" is the watchword in this discussion.

The Twelfth Step is used as the basis of a summary of the program of recovery, as our "insurance" in AA and as a way of living in keeping with normal human behavior and experience. The three parts of the Twelfth Step are discussed separately.

1. Spiritual experience is discussed as sudden conversion to a new way of life or the more common result of the cumulative effects of all experiences in working at the program which result in a personality change. Continuance of spiritual experience is emphasized.

2. Making calls on prospective members is cited as only one of the things considered in working with others. Personal aggrandizement, zeal to reform and increased membership are discussed as unsuitable reasons for making calls. Sincerity of purpose in helping others, humility in the knowledge of our own power to help, and confidence in our understanding of our capacities in AA are indicated as states of mind likely to help in working with others.

3. The last part of the Twelfth Step is discussed as a way of life that encompasses our motives, our methods and our accomplishments in A.A. It insures continuance of sobriety, happiness in what we do and peace of mind in the knowledge that we are progressing in our program of recovery with the help of a "power greater than ourselves."

L. S. L.
St. Paul, Minnesota

Little Rock Plan Gives Prospects Close Attention
September 1947

Greater Little Rock AA was seven years old last March and has helped establish most of the groups within the state. More than five hundred men and women have been initiated into AA through the Little Rock Approach Plan since its creation seven years ago when five men got together and began to use the book

Alcoholics Anonymous, which had just been published.

It is interesting to note that of these men, the founders of the movement here, all are alive and only one ever had a relapse. They are living, walking proof of the statement that "it works."

The Little Rock Plan was, we believe, the first of its kind in the country. By adhering strictly to the Plan hundreds have been brought into AA and because this group has kept accurate records and statistics, we can report that our success is better than the national average of 75 percent—or to put it another way, our "slip" record is lower than the 25 percent expected and reported from other groups over the country.

It is not easy to become a member of this group. When a person has expressed a desire to achieve sobriety and has had a sponsor appointed for him, he must leave his work or position for at least two weeks. Usually the prospect is required to spend that entire time within the confines of the club rooms, studying, preparing a case history, meeting and filling assignments laid out by the sponsor.

If, after two weeks, he has discharged his assignments to the satisfaction of his sponsor, he is brought before the executive committee and there his request for membership is presented by his sponsor in his presence. In some instances, because of the peculiarity of the case, he may not be admitted for varying periods as high as six months in some cases. However, if he is deemed eligible by the committee, he is brought before the next meeting, receives a warm welcome, is handed a copy of the "Approach Program" and the Twelve Steps.

This is not all, however. We do not simply say, "Now here you are, you have had it all, go your way, and may God bless you." No, we do not cut him off in mid-air, so to speak. We give him a small diary and ask that each day thereafter for twenty-eight days, he record his impressions of the day, any event, whether a happy one or a sad one, and enter therein, "I have not taken a drink this day," and sign his name.

At the end of this period he returns the diary to the club, is again welcomed and is admitted to full membership, the privilege of the ballot and an unrestricted part in the activities of the Fellowship. He is then assigned to a squad, given some definite task, and encouraged to work, guided by some older member, with new prospects.

In dealing with the new person, there are other procedures. First of all, in addition to being required to adhere strictly to the assignments required by his sponsor, he serves his apprenticeship in what is known as "The Prospect Squad." Here he learns from a squad leader various phases of the work of AA, mingles with other neophytes, hears their experiences and contributes his own. If he needs guidance or advice this is where he gets it, along with other newcomers, seeking the way out.

There is the "Slip Squad," where the member who has suffered a setback, no matter how severe or how light, must serve from two weeks to six months before he is again recognized as a full-fledged member. Often the slippee is assigned tougher, more strenuous assignments than when he first was admitted. Here he discusses the slip freely with those who, like himself, have "missed the boat" somewhere down the line. He tries to find out why he made the mistake and learns again that "to err is only human" and that a slip in the beginning is not uncommon, certainly not fatal.

The executive committee is comprised of representatives from each squad. The squads meet once a week on nights other than the regular meeting and transact actual AA business.

We spend much time in planning and executing the new member's graduation from the freshman stage. We carry him slowly and carefully through the "Prospect Squad"; admit him to membership; keep our contacts with him through that critical period, the first month or so, through his daily diary; put him in a squad after he becomes a full member and then if he slips, put him through again (and again if necessary) by way of the "Slip Squad."

Credit is due the State Hospital and Fort Roots, one of the Southwest's largest veterans' hospitals, where we have complete cooperation from the entire staff of doctors and psychiatrists. From Fort Roots especially, come more and more prospects, having been told by the psychiatrists, "We can do nothing more for you, your best bet is AA. It works." The courts of law in Arkansas in general and Little Rock in particular without exception lend a willing ear and helping hand to unfortunates who stand before the court and even so much as intimate that they would like to quit drinking. While we have gone far and progressed much, no small amount of credit is due to all these factors plus the attitude of all businessmen of this city.

G. H. B.
Little Rock, Arkansas

The Topic Is Change
February 2001

M y home group is Lambda AA, here in Beaumont, Texas. In 1984, the founders of our group chose the eleventh letter of the Greek alphabet because it is the symbol of freedom for gays and lesbians. However, while most of our members are gay or lesbian, we welcome everyone. The only requirement for membership is a desire to stop drinking.

Some of our members have many years of sobriety, while others are brand new. But in keeping with the principle "One Day at a Time," we are fond of noting that whomever got up first that day has the most sobriety.

Over the years, we have had many memorable meetings. Three stand out in my memory. When I was new to the program, a young man in the last stages of AIDS celebrated his first sobriety birthday. He spoke of his battle to give up alcohol and drugs and of the many blessings God had bestowed upon him. His gratitude was manifest, despite the ravages of his disease. AA had given him more than sobriety; it had given him acceptance. It had given him serenity. It was a privilege to be there that night.

Several years ago, another member suffered serious health problems. When she got out of the hospital, she was unable to leave her apartment. So we brought the meeting to her. We crowded into her living room. She was propped up on a sofa and was very weak. When the chairperson asked if anyone had a topic, she spoke up from the corner and suggested "gratitude." It was a marvelous meeting and provided me with much-needed perspective. We continued to converge on her apartment for a meeting once a week or so, and after a few months, celebrated her thirty-fifth AA birthday with her. As she spoke that night, I realized that she had been working her program throughout her illness. This took courage, but it also took a good program. Imagine our joy as her health returned for a while, and she was able to rejoin us.

Then there was our group's tenth anniversary meeting, a Lambda Birthday. We were able to rent a large room from a local charity and the city, and thirty-four gay men and lesbians came for a great meal and a candlelight meeting. Among those present were several of our group's founders, still sober after many years.

Nevertheless, in the last two years, we have confronted a serious problem: declining attendance. This was a problem for us because we are a small group. We held numerous group consciences to discuss this. We tried Big Book studies, "Twelve and Twelve" studies, videos, and speaker meetings. Nothing helped.

As we went through the process of a group inventory, we gradually realized there were two issues: first, we needed to change meeting places; and second, each of us needed to reach out more to other suffering alcoholics.

Change or some version of it became a frequent topic at meetings. We all came to realize that change was healthy and needed, although I have to admit throughout this, I behaved like the alcoholic I was, am, and forever will be. Until matters reached a desperate stage, I was unwilling to consider any change. I was the same way when I was drinking: I was not going to change even though it was apparent to all but me that serious changes were long overdue.

Finally, we all let go and let God. Last night, we held our first meeting in our beautiful new quarters. Two of our group celebrated birthdays and sixteen of us were present. Sixteen is a crowd for us.

Our old (and beloved by me) meeting place was only part of the problem. We were the rest. I can speak only for myself, but I had ceased attending other meetings and went only to Lambda. I had largely stopped reaching out to newcomers and others in the program. My complacency was overwhelming. It is a tribute to the cunning, baffling, and powerful nature of alcoholism that throughout this time, I thought I was working a good program. It took only a few meetings at other groups for me to grasp how dangerous my complacency was to my sobriety. I am grateful that God gently reminded me of the Twelfth Step.

As I write, I do not know whether Lambda AA will survive. That is in God's hands, not mine. I am going to do my part by attending Lambda and other meetings, by sponsoring, by giving my phone number to newcomers, by going out for coffee instead of rushing home to watch ESPN. In short, I am going to try working all Twelve Steps for a change.

Bob B.
Beaumont, Texas

Rekindling the Fire
August 1992

During a recent home group inventory, someone asked, "Where have all the old-timers gone?" After several possibilities were discussed, someone suggested that we conduct an old-timers meeting in place of one of our regularly scheduled Sunday night meetings. We all thought it was a great idea, and each of us made a personal commitment to invite an old-timer or two to that meeting. We selected the Sunday two weeks away.

Time passed unnoticed as we got our invitations out. We believed that if we attracted at least six to eight old-timers we would have accomplished quite a lot.

The meeting day finally arrived. I pulled into the parking lot of the church where we have our meetings, and I could not find a parking spot. My initial thought was that a church function was also going on. Then I began to recognize many old faces I had grown to love over past years. I felt the giddiness of a schoolboy going off to summer camp, and the anticipation and excitement of recapturing "the old days."

It became obvious to me that the God of our understanding had worked one more of his many miracles on that day. Word of the meeting had spread so widely that the large turnout forced us to move to a much larger room to accommodate everyone.

Other members of my home group appeared to be in a mixed state of shock and awe. Our typical greeting to one another as we tried to keep up with the coffee demand was, "I can't believe this!"

The meeting went on and I was able to hear and enjoy the messages of old: singleness of purpose, one alcoholic helping another, home group, the experiences of working the Steps, their own introduction to service work. And, oh! those wonderful stories of how it used to be.

It didn't take long to become intensely aware that something significantly spiritual was taking place in that parish hall. I was seeing a glow in old-timers' eyes that had seemed to be missing for such a long time. New meaning and zest appeared in their messages. Relationships were being rekindled, some dormant over 40 years! Most refreshing was the mutual respect and dignity felt throughout the hall in that fellowship of alcoholics, reminiscent of the personal stories described in our beloved Big Book.

After two hours we were only at 19 years of sobriety, with many more left to speak. So a group conscience was taken: we all agreed that something wonderful was taking place and that we would continue the old-timers meeting on a quarterly basis, to pick up where we had left off.

As the meeting came to a conclusion, the old-timers registration sheet was tabulated and we were able to announce that with seventy-five AAs signing in, we had enjoyed the experience, strength, and hope of over 744 years of continuous sobriety! It was truly a meeting that will be remembered and talked about for a long time to come.

My home group is not alone in asking where the old-timers have gone. The theme of the 1992 General Service Conference is "AA's Message in a Changing World." Question #2 of the Conference Workshop Questionnaire asks, "Why are so many old-timers leaving AA?"

The experience my home group would like to pass on is this: Instead of debating why so many old-timers are leaving, maybe our time would be better spent in taking more responsibility and letting the old-timers know how much AA wants and needs them; and by creating and maintaining environments and meetings that are attractive to *their* recovery.

Anonymous
Vancouver, Washington

Meeting in the Middle
May 1988

I am an alcoholic, and I would like to share with you the experience of my group in dealing with some of the opportunities we have had in regard to friends outside of AA and the solutions reached by an informed group conscience. (This article has been read to the group and is an "approved" version of an informed group conscience.)

Because of the location of our group (near to downtown in a major city), our experience is mainly with two groups of friends outside of AA: (1) folks sent by the court, and (2) busloads of treatment center or halfway house folks. Some in each of these groups are obviously (to us "experts") alcoholic, but many of them do not know or believe it—yet.

Here are some of the ways we handle folks with court or parole papers:

1. All attendance papers are given to the chairperson before the meeting starts. This is announced before the Preamble or

"How It Works" is read. This is our way of cooperating with the courts, in that a meeting is not the last ten minutes of the hour.

2. Papers are returned after the meeting is over, signed by the chairperson.

3. No papers are signed for those who are drunk or disruptive.

4. Court-assigned folks are invited to attend all open meetings (a schedule of our meetings is on the board, and is also announced at the beginning of the meeting) and our closed meetings if they feel they have a problem with booze (these meetings are also on the board and included in the announcement).

Treatment centers and halfway houses present a different opportunity. Many of the patients have problems with both alcohol and drugs other than alcohol. However, and we have found this to be true with the young people, many can only relate to their "drug" problem or their "addiction." We have had busloads of such folks sent by the drunk farms (I am a graduate of one of these places, and so happy that it was there in 1973 and made AA available) to our closed meetings where they denied being alcoholic and proceeded to address their drug problem. This was very disconcerting to those of us who were there to grow in sobriety and to follow the Third and Fifth Traditions. Our group solution was to ask one of our members to contact the outside agencies in this manner:

1. A warm and loving call to the center stating that our group conscience policy designates that closed meetings are for people with alcohol problems, and other problems just as long as one of these is booze. He explained that their clients without alcohol-related problems would be asked to leave closed meetings.

2. At the beginning of each closed meeting, the chairperson introduces her/himself as "an alcoholic" and asks that any other alcoholics in the room please signify by raising their hands. The chairperson asks those who do not raise their hands if they are there because they feel they are powerless over alcohol. If the

answer is no (many new candidates for Al-Anon have wandered into the "wrong" room and were relieved when shown their meeting place), they are asked to come back to our open meetings and the schedule is given to them. As of this date, no one has been asked to do that. A group conscience meeting voted that no measures to "oust" a person would be used, but the chairperson would certainly not call upon that person to share experience, strength, and hope.

Other fellowships have not been a problem with us, as we encourage anyone with other problems to attend our open meetings, or in a closed meeting to limit sharing to discussion of their alcohol-related problem.

This has been the experience of our group.

Anonymous
Dallas, Texas

My Ideal Group
November 1962

One of the fine old groups in my area is having a discussion meeting at which the subject is "My Idea of the Ideal AA Group." This is a group which I am seldom able to attend, but this challenging subject has moved me to a lot of reflection. Since I cannot go to the particular meeting I am going to record my random thoughts on paper, at least for my own benefit.

Here are my notions about the ideal AA group:

1. It should have lots of George. You know George. He is the fellow we "let do it." He just sort of moves in quietly and does things without being asked. Who wants to come early each week to get the chairs and other things arranged, frog up a pot of coffee for the ones who may want a spot before the meeting, and do a score of other little chores? Who wants to hang around each week to mop up, turn out the lights and lock the

door? George does it. He is cheerful, eager and friendly. Probably he is the only one who has spoken to each and every one in the room before the meeting breaks up. And is he appreciated? When we talk in high-sounding phrases about developing a fine sense of giving without hope of reward, why not save our breath and just point our index finger at George? You know something? He's the happiest guy around.

2. There should be a liberal sprinkling of dedicated old-timers—the finest symbols we have of what we like to call "good solid AA." They are the living proof to us all that this thing really works. Their mere presence inspires us all. They need our help too, let's not forget. They know better than do we, that this ailment of ours is chronic and incurable. That's why they are with us. Are we properly grateful to them?

3. There should be a sprinkling of dedicated high quality Twelfth Step workers, for to them we owe the constant trickle of newcomers. Why do they do so much sponsoring? Just because they are at all times ready, willing and able? No! It's because they have learned that we are helped through helping others, in direct proportion to the quality and effectiveness of the help we give. And so, when people begin to think of "Who would be a good man in this situation?" it's one of these.

4. There should be a steady trickle in that precious stream of newcomers. What could we possibly do without them? Where would we be without the Twelfth Step? In them we see the slow but certain miracle take place all over again under our very eyes. As we watch and help them grow, we literally start at the bottom of the ladder and each time we take those steps again our footing is a little surer, our understanding a little deeper and our surrender a little more complete. Only in this way do we make any progress at all.

5. There should be a plentiful supply of excellent leads by people of varying periods of sobriety, diverse drinking experiences, high and low and medium bottom drunks and other

distinctive characteristics— our leads, with the frank testimony of our members, represent the crux of our success.

6. There should be a liberal sprinkling of serious-minded, deep thinkers about our program. They make the comments that represent the frosting on our excellent cake. They induce us all to think and meditate and try to broaden our understanding. That is a must if we would make progress. Continuous striving for truth and understanding does not lead to all the answers but it does mean progress toward two other attainable goals. One is a knowledge of our true selves and hence some degree of humility. The other is that when we reach a maximum in understanding we know how very much we shall never understand. From there our faith and surrender can really take over. But we need these thoughtful people as a reminder, to keep us thinking.

7. There should be a group atmosphere which approaches perfection in tolerance, kindliness and understanding. The kind of atmosphere in which the sober alcoholic feels completely happy and at home. The kind of atmosphere in which each one keeps saying over and over to himself, subconsciously perhaps, Here I belong.

These are only a few of the attributes that I think of for the ideal group. And it occurs to me that I wouldn't fit at all. All these people would be further along than I am on the high road to sobriety. I might begin to think that I was as good as they were. I couldn't afford that. Who would I help? How could I stay sober without helping others?

Then too, on leads, I have found that I am helped by the lead that's off the beam. And what about the troublemakers? Could there be an AA group without one now and then? Would an AA group seem homelike if there weren't an occasional brush fire to put out? I don't know. I'm confused.

C. R.
Ashland, Ohio

A Light at the End of the Tunnel
October 1995

Our group holds three meetings a week at a local treatment facility. The oldest of the meetings is more than thirty-three years old; it began with the clear-cut goal of being the hand of AA reaching out to the alcoholics in the treatment center. With a firm foundation in AA basics, the meetings grew in size and number. Thousands of men and women became sober at these meetings.

However, as the dynamics of treatment changed over the years and as the numbers and types of alcoholics entering treatment changed, so did our meetings. The newcomers wanted to adjust the content of the meetings to suit their individual needs, not those of the group. I'm sad to say that I was one of the most vocal and persuasive of these young know-it-alls. Four years ago, as we newcomers vastly outnumbered the old-timers, and we made our displeasure known, the old-timers said, "Go for it. Try your new ideas. We'll see how long the group lasts."

Of course, we newcomers were sure our ideas were better. We made all of our meetings open meetings. We began attracting all sorts of people who had problems other than alcohol; often, alcohol was never discussed at the meetings. Slowly the old-timers stopped coming to our meetings altogether. And since few, if any, of the remaining chairpeople had sponsors or worked the Steps or read the Big Book, the meetings turned into bitch sessions and advice sessions rather than AA meetings.

Eventually attendance dwindled to a few people each week. Chairpeople couldn't be found or wouldn't show up. Intergroup attendance was spotty. And the money we collected rarely made it to the treasurer (an old-timer who couldn't bear seeing what had happened to this once-thriving group). Even I was disturbed at the lack of AA quality at these meetings, yet I couldn't quite figure out what had gone wrong. I began going to only one of the group's three meetings. (This soon became the only meeting I went to each week; you see, my style of AA didn't include finding a sponsor. I thought I could work the Steps on my own. And after nearly four years I was still on Step Three and couldn't understand why I was so miserable.) The treatment center was seriously considering throwing our group out; we really weren't fulfilling our mission and were probably doing more harm than good overall. It seemed that the old-timers' prophecy was coming true.

By the grace of God, last December marked a turning point for the Ray of Hope Group. Two men, one just a baby in this program, the other with a healthy sobriety of five years, committed themselves to helping the group. We made the decision that if in six months we couldn't turn Ray of Hope around, we'd end the group. Our Monday night meeting became a closed Step meeting based on the "Twelve and Twelve." The Wednesday night open speaker meeting began attracting good speakers with sobriety based on the basics of Alcoholics Anonymous. And the Friday closed discussion meeting stuck to Big Book topics. We went to the local intergroup meeting and acknowledged the mistakes our group had made, promising to stick to the basics if people would ask their group members to support us by attending a few of our meetings. Flyers were distributed. Service positions were filled. And a miracle began to take place.

Our group is bouncing back. Attendance is growing and a number of people have made Ray of Hope their home group. We're self-supporting through our own contributions. We're earning a reputation as a vibrant, good group of which to be a part. And the treatment center now considers our meetings a vital part of their patients' recoveries.

Which brings us to our Grapevine subscriptions. All of the group's trusted servants read Grapevine regularly; we feel it's a key part of our recovery. And since many of our group members are new to sobriety, we want to give them the opportunity to discover AA's meeting in print. Each month we will have two issues of Grapevine available for one dollar apiece. One of our Friday discussion meetings each month will revolve around that month's Grapevine. And we will be pushing subscriptions.

On a brief personal note, after those two men helped turn Ray of Hope around, they began working on me. I now have a wonderful sponsor and I'm diligently working the Twelve Steps. Thank God for this program and the miracles it inspires.

Stephanie J.
Fort Wayne, Indiana

In Order to Heal
May 2021

A friend asked me to help with moderating an inventory for a large AA group in a major city in our general service area. Both of us had some experience with moderating a group inventory, but we had only worked with much smaller groups.

I agreed to help, but like my friend I didn't feel confident moderating an inventory for such a large, well-established group. No one in the group could recall when they had had their last inventory. AA members often share about the importance of taking a personal inventory, but those same members often chafe at the idea of doing it for their group. Based on my experience with this group, it was apparent that it was sorely in need of an inventory.

The group's general service representative (GSR) spearheaded the inventory motion and conducted a survey of the members to identify problems and issues. Participation in the survey was overwhelming; the GSR had 25 pages of input from the members.

The GSR organized the issues by category and gave them to me and my friend to decide what questions we would ask using the AA Grapevine Traditions Checklist. Groups have the autonomy to decide how each will structure their inventory. Some use the questions suggested in "The A.A. Group" pamphlet, while others use the Twelve Traditions or the General Warranties of the Twelfth Concept as a guide. Some groups just choose questions relevant to their issues.

The survey results indicated a general lack of unity. Complaints about the group's rules and trusted servant requirements were common. Other problems included cliques, gossip and a lack of focus on newcomers.

I've heard it suggested that a group inventory should be taken on a regular basis and not only after things have gotten out of hand. My experience is that many groups don't consider having an inventory until they're in a lot of pain. What unity remained in this group was tenuous at best.

My friend and I came up with four questions for the inventory. The funny thing was that we only needed to ask one question. That was the first question of the checklist under Tradition One: Am I in my group a healing, mending, integrating person? Am I sometimes divisive? Do I ever gossip or take another member's inventory?

The questions focused the group's problems back on each individual member. We explored what part each individual played in the disunity that permeated this group. We used a sharing session model for the inventory and each person had two minutes to share. Members shared about taking responsibility for their actions and possible solutions for the group to consider.

The amazing thing was that the group followed up on the inventory and implemented some of the changes that were suggested. Just like in a personal inventory, the group members needed to look at their parts and identify their own character flaws in order to heal. The inventory was, in a real sense, a spiritual awakening that helped the group recover.

Woody R.
Stockton, California

A Place Called Home
Online Exclusive
October 2015

The Oxford dictionary defines "home" as "a place where something flourishes, is most typically found, or from which it originates." It makes sense to me to apply this definition to our concept of home group in AA. It is in our home group that we flourish in sobriety. It is where we really learn how to live, group up, give and share.

What makes a home group different from a regular meeting? A home group is where we are rooted. Our fellows know our story. This is where we celebrate, where we go to mourn and grieve when we have to, and it is where we simply show up for the newcomer on a regular basis.

I recently was given the opportunity to participate in a home group inventory and found it to be so much fun! Those who were interested gathered to ask questions about how we were doing as a group. We asked questions like:

- Are we doing enough to carry the message?
- What more can we do?
- Are we attracting a good cross section of our community?

We even looked at the kind of language that was being used at the meetings. As a group, we brainstormed ideas which were recorded and held for discussion at future business meetings. After a few hours, we all felt a great sense of group cohesion.

I would highly recommend this process to other groups. We used the pamphlet from G.S.O., "The A.A. Group."

I am so glad that I took the suggestion from my sponsor to get a home group. It's a place I love. It gives me a sense of belonging and the opportunity to be of service. It is through being of service that I have really grown in my sobriety. I was taught to see how I was needed, rather than what I needed.

I tell anyone who doesn't have a home group to find one. I tell them: "Commit! Get Involved! Be strong enough to be vulnerable! Let people know you." The experience of growing and flourishing to your maximum potential in sobriety is not to be missed. We get this when we come home to our home group.

So, let's plant seeds and watch them grow. It's our garden of sobriety. Happy gardening!

Brenda M.
Boise, Idaho

SECTION FOUR

The Traditions at Work

Psst! Hey, Buddy!
October 1985

Nobody wants to talk about the Traditions. "We don't want to hear about all the politics stuff! Let's talk recovery program!" Really?

What do we talk about when we take a newcomer to a meeting? We sure don't talk recovery program! Can you visualize a newcomer sitting, shaking, worried, fearful in the front seat of the car riding to his or her first meeting?

The AA sponsor announces, "We're going to help you recover from your alcoholism with this Twelve Step program. First, you'll admit you're powerless. Then, you'll surrender to God, take a moral inventory, and confess your faults."

The newcomer fumbles for the door handle. "Surrender to God? Confess my faults? Are you people some kind of religious nuts? Let me out of here!"

No, the AA sponsor talks soothingly about things like anonymity, no dues to pay, no bosses in AA, no affiliation with outside groups, no membership requirement except a desire to stop drinking—all to make our newcomer feel comfortable and protected. We talk Traditions to our people in AA long before we broach the sensitive subjects in the Steps.

We think AA will be around forever, but we have nothing to prove it—no AA buildings, towers, or monuments. We are no more permanent than the length of our office lease and the one year's prudent reserve in our treasury. Our groups are month-to-month tenants in churches and meeting halls. The clubhouses are not allied with AA; there, the groups rent meeting space only. The groups aren't well organized, have no bylaws or charters. Officers are elected for terms from six months to two years and resign at will. Meeting formats are loose and mostly unstructured. No policing force exists to make members conform to any rules or regulations.

AA does have a service structure, but it is an upside-down pyramid, with the groups in charge over the board of trustees. With groups as loosely designed as they are, one is tempted to think about comparison to the strength of a chain. If AA is as strong as its weakest group—just how well is AA equipped to survive?

What ever happened to the Washingtonian Society? In pre-Civil War days, they claimed half a million members who helped sober up other drunks. Abraham Lincoln gave a speech to them that we in AA treasure today. The Oxford Group, which sobered up Ebby T. to carry a message to our cofounder Bill W., is gone. Buchmanism, named for Frank Buchman, who started the Oxford Group, turned into Moral Rearmament; both are gone. Who is to say that AA won't have a similar obituary in some article about alcoholism treatment in the year 2085 AD?

Some groups have Tradition meetings. Formats vary. Two groups that we know of read and discuss a Tradition once a month. Another group reads the AA pamphlet, "The Twelve Traditions Illustrated" and discusses them during the meetings in November, Traditions month. Another group puts on the Traditions play (copies available through the AA General Service Office), which gives a hilarious look at the results of breaking the Traditions and opens the door to discussion and understanding by the members.

One longtime member of a group summed it all up when he said, "You know, I voted against these Tradition meetings. And I refused to comment during the discussion. But I have to admit that now we are doing the Traditions, I'm beginning to enjoy it!"

It's simple.

Informed members in AA will tell you that if groups follow the Traditions, AA will survive and grow and, for a long time to come, continue to carry the message to the alcoholic who still suffers.

N. A.
Wenonah, New Jersey

The Strength We Gained
January 1992

All members of our group agree that our Friday night Big Book Study Meeting is our lifeline. An old-time Big Book thumping meeting, it offers a clear and strong message of recovery through the Steps of Alcoholics Anonymous. Newcomers and old-timers alike come once and end up staying. We have nearly doubled our size in the last year. The foundation of our strength is our singleness of purpose. We rely on the Big Book totally. We focus only on the book, dealing with personal problems at the break.

But suddenly this powerful meeting was threatened with breakup due to an outside issue. We were a smoking meeting, dividing the room into smokers on one side, nonsmokers on the other. We had one fan, but in the winter we had to close the doors. It finally became unbearable and the nonsmokers had to take a stand: Go nonsmoking or we would start another meeting. I felt particularly bad because it was my allergies that had begun the fight.

Tempers flared for two weeks. Each faction barely spoke to the other. Many phone calls were made. There were angry conversations and much character assassination all the way around. But there were also many prayers said for the unity of the meeting.

The night of our group conscience meeting came. We were sitting around the tables glaring at one another. The chairperson—newly elected—was terrified. She didn't think she could keep the group in order. She opened with a passage from page 287 of *AA Comes of Age*, the one about personal sacrifice:

"When the first AA group took form, we soon learned a lot more about this. We found that each of us had to make willing sacrifices for the group itself, sacrifices for the common welfare. The group, in turn, found it had to give up many of its own rights for the protection and welfare of each member, and for AA as a whole. These sacrifices had to be made or AA could not continue to exist."

She also had the presence of mind to begin the discussion not with the smoking issue, but with the group inventory from the "Group Handbook."

As we read through the questions, the responses were at first slow in coming and the respondents' voices tense and hard. Yes, we were doing much to carry the message. Yes, we had a good cross section. We could do a little more in the way of public information, but we were very good, better than most groups in our area, at making the newcomer feel welcome.

Suddenly the tension was split open. We began to laugh and joke with one another as was our former custom. In an instant—seemingly at the same time—we were all struck with the same idea. This is the best meeting in the world. The love that we all have for one another came flooding out. We finished the inventory with a feeling of euphoria. But we still had to discuss the smoking issue. The discussion began and the smokers still didn't want to give up their "pleasure." But some of the most vehemently opposed had changed their minds. Oddly enough it was because of the paragraph from *AA Comes of Age*, which some of the smokers had proposed reading to the nonsmokers to show how they should be willing to make some sacrifices to keep the meeting together. By this time, too, some of the nonsmokers were willing to try to continue with the smoke while thinking of ways to alleviate the problem.

Then a relative newcomer stood up (it was someone we had "picked up" at a treatment center, who claims we saved his life) and said simply, "I'm frightened. If this meeting is threatened with a breakup because of my Pall Malls"—he threw them down on the table dramatically—"then I say they're not worth it." He had spoken for all of us. We were all frightened.

Someone offered us a smoke-eater, but I said that unless there was no smoke in the room, I would not be able to come back, because of increasing illness due to smoke. Someone else had problems breathing, too.

The time came for the vote. Tears came to my eyes. If the vote went one way this was my last meeting here. I was crushed. I loved this meeting but my illness dictated my actions. The chair called for the vote—very few hands went up. But then a few more went up and then almost all hands were raised. It was 19-3 in favor of nonsmoking (the nonsmokers were outnumbered in attendance that night 18-8). We were bonded by the Higher Power. We were not angry at each other anymore. The seemingly unbridgeable rent had been repaired. The unity of our group was more important to us than our personal pleasures.

Even the non-huggers hugged that night. At our customary coffee hour after the meeting we stayed longer than usual, needing to bask in the warmth we felt that night. The feeling continues and all differences seem to have been healed. We have moved on, despite having had several people slip. But those of us who stay know the strength we gained from that controversy. And others know only that we are a strong meeting.

We learned a great lesson that night. Personal recovery really does depend on AA unity—and the AA Traditions are a vital tool in helping us keep our meetings in good health.

B. v. M.
Portsmouth, Rhode Island

Whose Turf Are We On?
March 1986

The noon closed discussion meeting I went to today is a good example of some of the confusion within the Fellowship. Our group meets four times a week in the heart of the downtown Denver business district; three meetings are closed, one is open.

We have from ten to forty people at our meetings, which are all discussion meetings. We have one regular member who hasn't had a drink in eighteen years, a dozen with over five years of sobriety, and plenty of people with less than five years. We have Catholics, Protestants, Jews, blacks, whites, Spanish-Americans, gays, straights, dually addicted and "boozers-only," professionals, skid-row types, etc. It isn't a perfect group, but it's been getting better and better. More and more members are talking about the Steps, sponsorship, and the Traditions; more and more are focusing on the reason why we need to "keep comin' back."

Our group is quite a melting pot of approaches to the program—everything from "just don't drink and go to meetings," to "spiritual thugs" who try to cram the Big Book down others' throats. It's the only game in town in downtown Denver at noon on Monday, Tuesday, Wednesday, and Friday.

Our group, like the rest of AA, is hurting from the drug and pill controversy. Today we talked about the First Tradition, and that issue came up. There are three viewpoints within our group, as there are, I think, in AA:

1.   Right wing—"I don't want to hear a @#%¢*! thing about your *@#$! drug problem at an AA meeting!" These people have already begun to "go underground" and have a few by-invitation-only meetings which are not listed in the local meeting schedule.

2.   Center—"Feel free to *mention* drugs and pills in connection with your drinking, but please focus on our common problem—the first *drink*, and on our common solution, a power greater than ourselves. AA has a different focus from Al-Anon, NA, EA, PA, GA, etc."

3.   Left wing—"AA must change. Alcoholism and drug addiction are the same problem. People should feel free to talk about drugs and pills as much as they want to at AA meetings." Many who hold this viewpoint are alumni of one of our local treatment centers.

I believe I am in the center on this question. Some feel that "God will take care of AA and the problem will take care of itself." I think this usually really means "I can't handle controversy, and when the right wing in AA dies off, the new generation of AAs will be predominantly dually addicted people." But AA is not about numbers, being all things to all people, increased subscription rates for Grapevine, or increased contributions to GSO. *Each group has but one primary purpose—to carry its message to the alcoholic who still suffers.*

There are indeed more dually addicted people at AA meetings. They should be welcomed. The focus of an Alcoholics Anonymous meeting should remain alcohol. There are so many dually addicted people today that they should be able to start plenty of NA or PA meetings to focus on drugs and pills, so that the nonalcoholic drug addict has a place to help him recover, too. In Denver, this didn't start happening until two or three years ago. Fortunately, there are now more than forty NA meetings a week in the Denver area.

Today's meeting, however, made me sad. Some of the right-wingers expressed so much anger and venom about people talking about their !$*%¢ drug problems at AA meetings that some of the dually addicted newcomers were quite shaken. We have a group conscience meeting next Wednesday and, frankly, I fear that the left-wingers will show that "No one can run us out!" by "packing" the group conscience with dually addicted people who don't usually come.

Meanwhile, those of us in the middle wonder what will become of our group, and of AA in general.

Anonymous
Denver, Colorado

Citizens of the World
April 1998

The Monday evening meeting started off as an "informational meeting" for people with drunk-driving citations. It was conceived and designed by our local Public Information/Co-operation with the Professional Community (PI/CPC) committee. It offered an AA meeting for those who needed attendance slips signed. At that time, many groups refused or were reluctant to sign them.

In keeping with the autonomy referred to in Tradition Four, the format was a bit different from local AA group meetings. It began with a Statement of Purpose and a description of AA meetings—closed or open, speaker or discussion—and most of the readings came from literature designed for beginners ("This is AA," "44 Questions"). A speaker with some drunk-driving experience was invited to share, and the meeting ended—instead of opened—with the Serenity Prayer. It served its purpose for three years, until some of the groups became more tolerant and welcomed those requiring slips to be signed.

When the PI/CPC committee relinquished sponsorship of the meeting, several AA members decided to maintain it as a bona fide AA group. The format was changed to conform with other local group meetings. The group continued to meet in the same place, the conference room of a small, satellite medical center, where everything except the coffee and literature was permanently set up. It was easy to "Keep It Simple," with but a few active home group members participating.

The group continued for several years with the least amount of organization until the administration of the medical center notified the group secretary of its plans to renovate. We were told we wouldn't be able to meet there for quite a while. Should we cancel the meeting or look for another landlord?

A phone call to a church located just up the road from the former meeting place produced some unexpected results. "We've been thinking of having a group such as yours," said the church secretary. "I'll check with our board and the pastor and get back to you." Two days later, the group was invited (not just authorized) to meet in the church on the very next Monday and every Monday thereafter. We were elated!

Only then did we realize that now there were more responsibilities: keeping the key, setting up the chairs and tables, cleaning up and taking down, locking up, etc. Three or four different table arrangements were tried. We needed a podium and more literature and most of all, more members! A more definitive group conscience began to form. The group wanted to leave the meeting place better than it found it; we didn't want to jeopardize our good relations with the landlord. In so doing, the members benefited as much as the group did. As Bill W.

once wrote, "In AA we aim not only for sobriety—we try again to become citizens of the world that we rejected, and of the world that once rejected us."

Along with the autonomy accorded to every AA group in Tradition Four, come certain responsibilities, one of which I'd venture to say is a good relationship with our landlords.

Lois C.
Pittsburgh, Pennsylvania

Courage to Change
September 1988

When we first moved to Columbia, Tennessee, in the winter of 1984, there were only two AA meetings a week. They were both held in a small house called the Friendship Club.

This house had been purchased by a small group of recovering alcoholics and paid for by each one setting aside the price of a pint of whiskey per week. This was all done in a spirit of love and service.

Over the next few years, I had the pleasure of watching this small group grow from those two meetings to the fourteen meetings a week that it currently has. Membership in the group grew from about ten to over sixty. What a joy it was to see so many people getting sober.

There was, however, one group of people who were obviously absent from this fellowship—Blacks.

My wife was sponsoring one Black woman, Annie, who attended regularly. But others who came to our meetings seemed to drift away as quietly and suddenly as they had arrived. When I talked to Annie about the problem we had with attracting Blacks, she shared her personal experience with me. She explained that she felt uncomfortable when she first came to our group because of her "uniqueness." But because of her determination to stay sober, she kept coming back.

It became obvious to me that prejudice and alcohol were both holding many of God's children in bondage.

Like most small rural communities, the majority of Blacks seem to live on one side of town. From where I live, it is necessary for me to drive through that neighborhood to get to a meeting, and each time I would express to my wife that "someone" should get a meeting started in the Black neighborhood.

It was a Wednesday night in December 1986 that I made a phone call in response to a message left on the AA answering machine. My call was to a Black man who was feeling all the misery and helplessness that alcoholics are so familiar with. I got to share with this man my experience, strength, and hope. Almost an hour later, he agreed to attend an AA meeting the next night. I made arrangements to pick him up at his house at 7:30 PM.

I arrived at Willie's house fifteen minutes early just in case he decided to back out at the last minute. I thought I was being clever. When blowing my horn didn't produce any results, I went to the door determined that this man was going to a meeting. Standing on the porch, I could hear the mournful cry of a woman inside the house. Finally a young woman came to the door. I introduced myself and explained why I was there. I was not prepared for the shock I received when she told me that Willie was dead.

I stood on the porch that night and cried like a baby. Not because of any sense of loss, since I had never met Willie, but because of the guilt and shame that overwhelmed me. Another life had been claimed by alcohol—only one block from where I had so many times expressed that "someone" needed to get a meeting started for these people.

I went on to my meeting that night. When Annie and my wife arrived, I told them about my experience. I asked Annie if there was any building where we could start a meeting in the Black neighborhood.

That's all it took for Annie. The seed had been planted and God took over. That Sunday night, the first meeting of the Courage to Change Group was held in a Black neighborhood, in a Black Baptist church, chaired by a Black alcoholic. Twenty-three people showed up.

As GSR of my home group, I queried the group conscience at our monthly business meeting if the group would consider sponsoring

this new group. It was unanimous. We immediately furnished literature and support for the new group.

My wife and I are now members of the Courage to Change Group
and Annie was elected GSR. I regret that someone had to die in order
that we may be here but I find great consolation in knowing that we
exist because of a genuine love and concern for the alcoholic who still
suffers. I am also very proud to be a member of a group that didn't
begin with a grudge and a coffeepot.

Charles M.
Columbia, Tennessee

Group Inventory: How Are We Doing?
July 1952

The Twelve Steps point the way to an ever richer personal sobriety. They are intended to be practiced principally by individuals, each in his own way, but they should also have a
bearing on group thought and action. Should we not "practice these
principles in all our (group) affairs?"

The Twelve Traditions, while they have certain implications for the
individual, apply with special emphasis to the group and to AA as a
whole. Five of them make specific reference to the group. They con-
stitute a charter that enumerates objectives, powers, and restrictions.
Their proper application is essential to the success and growth of AA
and indirectly of the alcoholic who still suffers.

Like an individual, a group has abilities and limitations; an overall attitude that may or may not be healthy; and a drive that may
be strong or wavering. A group can become smug and lazy or can
increase in vigor and spirit. It can succeed, do a so-so job, or fail, as
some have.

To fulfill its responsibility and achieve success commensurate
with the sum total of its members' talents, a group should practice
those Steps and apply those Traditions which are obvious guides to

group endeavor. For example, just as periodic inventory is essential to personal growth, so also is group inventory vital to maximal group success.

Periodically a group should ask itself, perhaps in a closed meeting, "How are we doing?" The question can be rephrased in many ways. Here are a few variations. Each group can doubtless add to the list.

1. (a) Are we experiencing a normal growth for a group our size and for the population density of our area?

(b) Are we getting a cross-section of our population, male and female, or are we getting men only? Does our membership consist solely of the upper crust to the complete neglect of those on the other side of the tracks? Or, are we failing to reach a fair share of those in the higher income brackets?

(c) The Eleventh Tradition states that "our public relations policy is based on attraction rather than promotion..." Do we construe that to mean that we are relieved of all active effort? That, therefore, there is no meaning in the Fifth Tradition which declares without qualification, "Each group has but one primary purpose—to carry its message to the alcoholic who still suffers?" Have we ever reflected on the meaning of the words "to carry"? Do they mean merely to sit back and wait for the telephone to ring? Is that the way Bill and Dr. Bob got the first hundred?

(d) Do we have the best meeting place available, taking into account all relevant factors? Or is it the same as when our group was started, a bit on the crummy side with little appeal for new prospects? Do we continue it because of necessity, deliberate choice, or through sheer inertia with no one undertaking the task of finding something better?

(e) Do we maintain an adequate supply of literature and do we keep it on a table near the door where members and visitors can see it both on arriving and leaving? Or do we keep it on a table in the front of the room even though we know that only a minority will come forward to browse through it?

Just what have we done about carrying the message?

2. (a) How effective is our sponsorship system? Do our sponsors have a real sense of responsibility and unending perseverance? Do we see that each new member has a sponsor, or at least someone responsible for getting him to meetings during that early period when he so easily may have a change of heart? Or do we say, "He knows where we are. If he wants it, he can come and get it"?

Do we ever analyze the reason for failure in our sponsorship efforts? Or do we always excuse ourselves by saying, "He isn't ready for it"? How can we be so sure he was not ready for it? Can we be certain that some other sponsor might not have succeeded? If that be the case, who is really responsible for the failure? Did we really do our best?

(b) Without our knowing it, could a scared newcomer drop into one of our open meetings and slip out again, perhaps never to return? Do we make a point of visiting with newer members and strangers at the meetings or do we tend to hang together in impenetrable cliques?

3. (a) Do we lend support in proportion to our means to our Intergroup office and to the Foundation [now the AA General Service Office]?

Intergroup and the Foundation [GSO] do our Twelfth Step work on a regional and international basis, respectively. Do we expect them to do this broader type of Twelfth Step work for us but withhold our enthusiastic cooperation and support?

(b) Have we made a sustained effort to interest everyone in subscribing to Grapevine? Our international journal is the clearing house for ideas. Thoughts arising in Los Angeles, Dallas or London are channeled to every group and ultimately to every member. It would be interesting to compare the success of various groups with Grapevine circulation, not that Grapevine produced the success, but that subscriptions may be evidence of vigor and activity which result in success.

(c) Do we have men or women in the group who by education and experience are capable of writing Grapevine articles of high quality, and if so do we encourage them to produce such articles so that the group can make some creative contribution to AA as a whole? Or do we just "let George do it"?

4. Do we select our officers with care? Or do we haphazardly bring the matter up in a meeting and if someone nominates Joe Doakes the nominations are closed and Joe, regardless of his lack of qualifications, becomes the goat—or does the group and the alcoholics who still suffer? Should not a nominating committee of responsible and experienced members give serious thought to the selection of the best possible slate of officers and present it to the group for its consideration?

Do we regard an officership as a chore to unload on some unfortunate member not present at the election, or as an honor, challenge, and a unique opportunity to do Twelfth Step work of a high order?

Here are four questions (with subdivisions, perhaps), but should not each group raise them from time to time? There are numerous others which can be asked by any group that wishes to take an inventory that is both searching and fearless. It would be interesting to devote a closed meeting to a review of the Steps and the Traditions to see how each of them applied to the group.

Groups in different stages of development will, of course, ask different questions. Perhaps in rare instances a group of long standing, like some individuals, may have to start at the beginning with the First Step admit that our group life has become unmanageable. Then what? Naturally, the Second Step.

Anonymous
Scarsdale, New York

How Autonomous Can You Be?
August 1960

Apopular cartoon by William Steig shows a dour little man huddled inside a box. The caption reads: "People are no damn good."

I was reminded of this cartoon as some delegates to the Tenth General Service Conference of AA last April mentioned groups in their areas which decline to participate in the worldwide services of Alcoholics Anonymous because—so the report went—they prefer to be *autonomous.* Obvious though the answer may be to many, still the question arises: "Does group autonomy mean group isolation?" Or, does group autonomy mean nonparticipation in any but local AA activities?

Everybody agrees that self-government of the local group is an essential AA principle. One of the most common daily activities of staff members at the General Service Office is the reminding of groups that a particular question raised in correspondence can only be settled by the group itself. GSO does offer advice as requested; it does prepare literature in which group experience with certain problems is made available to all; GSO speakers when invited to area meetings regularly present not their own opinions but the varied experiences throughout the AA world as reported to GSO.

Self-government is so deeply imbedded in the AA Traditions after twenty-five years that it is far from needing defense. On the contrary, here—as through all AA and indeed all human affairs—*easy* does it applies. Autonomy, like all other good things, can be carried to excess. Autonomy can become isolation; the self-respecting individual—independent, self-supporting, deciding for himself what is right and good— can (as he carries his independence to an extreme) become the dour, sour little man in the box, cherishing the thought that "people are no damn good," a thought which, carried to its logical conclusion, includes himself.

In this respect the group is like the individual. It must be responsible for the management of its own affairs; elect its officers and representatives; raise its own finances; provide its own meeting place; conduct its meetings as it sees fit; develop its own program of Twelfth Step work and sponsorship; work out its own arrangements with other groups and individuals in the community.

But it should not try to operate in a vacuum. No one "got AA" in isolation. Each member of the group is sober today because some other individual "carried the message." And no individual stays sober in AA by himself but as a member of a group. Whether it be a local group, his own "correspondence group," or the larger group of AA as a whole. No group developed of itself and by itself. No single group is responsible for the development of the principles we live by—the three legacies of Recovery, Unity and Service; no group can handle the thousands of inquiries which flow in each month, assign AA members to call on new prospects, provide for the translation of the AA message into other languages, keep in touch with hospital and prison groups, advise press, radio, and TV on AA ideas and procedures, keep in touch with the Loners and Internationalists—no group is wise enough, big enough, wealthy enough to do the total AA job today.

Paul Tillich, recognized as one of the great philosophers and theologians of our times, says that every individual must have the "courage to be"—courage to be himself and courage to be part of something else. The man who does not have the courage to be himself, to stand for something, to preserve his identity and to refuse to become a slave to either tradition or custom ceases to be a man and flees from life's realities into some larger group where he may be supported; the man who does not have the courage to be part of something else isolates himself from the stream of life and deprives the society of which he is a part of his interest, support, and ideas.

Both types of participation are needed, Tillich says, for the full life. This idea can be applied equally to the groups in AA. They must have the courage to be themselves, to stand on their own feet, to meet the problems of relations with other groups and with outside agencies without fear and without arrogance. Many of the problems forwarded to GSO will disappear as local groups become truly autonomous—in actuality as well as in Tradition.

But just as individuals in AA need each other's support, so the groups need a sense of fellowship with others in the AA way of life.

Just what damage is done when a group chooses to withdraw from participation in the whole AA movement, to function only in its own community, for the benefit of its own members? AA as a whole loses because it is deprived of the knowledge of local thinking, local solutions to local problems. Virtually all AA problems exist at the local level; there are a few national or state situations, but most of our difficulties arise out of local developments. The group which refuses to share its experiences with others makes it just so much harder for the group in the neighboring town or nearby state—or across the world—to handle similar situations when they arise.

A secondary—but just as damaging—loss is to the group itself. Just as individual thinking on the Twelve Steps and the Twelve Traditions can become warped if the individual does not occasionally check his thinking against that of his brother in AA, so group thinking can get "off the beam" on strange and even weird tangents, sometimes producing interpretations which most other AAs would question. Contacts with other groups and with the movement as a whole can contribute much toward the overall unity of the larger group conscience of AA as a whole.

Thus are we bound up together in a Fellowship which depends for its strength and performance on the loving attachment of all its groups and individual members, one with another. And thus do we see that autonomy, if carried to an extreme, can make of AA a fragmented affair, limited to the strength of each local group, unable to speak with a united voice to the millions who still desperately need to hear the message we have to carry.

The local group which withdraws into outer space punishes itself and its members as well. It becomes inbred. By its very act of isolation from others in AA it tends likewise to isolate itself from society and often stops carrying the message, being content to remain a tiny self-admiration society of recovered drunks. It deprives its members of satisfaction in the achievements of AA at home and abroad. Is a new group helped to get started somewhere? The isolated group has had no hand in it. If the very exciting news of the translation of *Alcoholics Anonymous* in still another foreign tongue is reported the isolated group can feel no sense of shared responsibility. If a sailor, struggling against heavy odds to keep sober on the beach in Yokohama, finds help through a Japanese AA group or a loner in a prospector's cabin miles from civilization keeps clear of the bottle because of a stream of friendly letters from GSO; if alcoholics in a state prison or mental hospital are helped to prepare for sobriety in the outside world by GSO's encouraging support to the institutional groups; if these and thousands of other efforts in the world struggle against alcoholism succeed inch by painful inch; if all these things in which AA members rejoice come to pass—the isolated group can take no joy in them if, in truth, it thinks about them or even hears about them.

The strength of AA sobriety rests on the shared experience. AA members and groups have differed in the past, differ today, and will differ tomorrow. Through argument we grow in wisdom and strength. But we shall fall apart if every individual or every group pulls out over each disagreement with some action or viewpoint—whether of another individual, another group, or AA as a whole through its General Service Conference.

The Traditions stress this thought in many ways: "...there is but one ultimate authority—a loving God as He may express Himself in our group conscience." "Each group should be autonomous except in matters affecting other groups or A.A. as a whole." "Every A.A. group ought to be fully self-supporting..."

Just as one of the horrors of our drinking days was loneliness, so one of the greatest joys of our recovery has been the love and support we have found from others in AA. As free individuals and members of AA's autonomous groups, we ought always to remember that our recovery depended on the support of others, as does the continuance of our sobriety. Simple gratitude compels us all to be mindful of the needs of others and to work in the ways and through the means developed by the AA movement to try to reach some of the millions of our fellow alcoholics who are still suffering in the hell from which we have escaped.

J. P. L.
Paterson, New Jersey

With the Best of Intentions
March 1993

The cooperative link between AA and hospitals and treatment facilities has been a lifesaver to thousands. Yet is it possible that, with the best of intentions, we as a Fellowship have gone too far in accepting the hospitality of treatment facilities?

I was all of four months without a drink and a member of an AA group that held its weekly Saturday night meeting in a rehab center in which, it so happens, I'd spent thirty-five days, when I first heard someone say, "AAs should not hold their home group meetings in treatment facilities. The group perpetuates a mixed message, and eventually you'll lose your autonomy." With bruised feelings, I dismissed this individual as one of those bleeding deacons I'd heard about—a purist.

Then, as he passed by on the way out, he looked me straight in the eye and said, "Unless a group conforms to AA's spiritual principles, it will die. Without groups, we will die. I doubt that there is even one Tradition this group does not violate." At the time, the group was about five years old. Within another three, his prophecy about this group's future was fulfilled.

Tradition Five tells us that the primary purpose of a group is "to carry its message to the alcoholic who still suffers." The primary purpose of a group that meets in a treatment facility is no different. But what is actually put into practice?

My home group was originally formed not because a couple of sober drunks got together to fill a need, but at the request of an alcoholism professional who, with the best of intentions, felt that the patients in the rehab would benefit from having an AA group hold its regular meeting at the facility. True enough. But this raised the possibility of clients assuming that AA and "treatment" were one and the same. Or even that AA meetings were somehow part of the insurance requirements.

"As a group we can do anything we want!" I cringe when I recall how often that fell out of my mouth during my first year in AA. "We're cooperating" was another phrase I repeated but did not understand.

Our literature table was filled with every kind of recovery book in print. Somewhere in the midst, you *might* find AA's Conference-approved literature.

As with most large rehabs, there was an "alumni" association, which had annual dues and held social events like dances, fishing trips, and softball games. These were announced right along with the intergroup secretary's reports as a part of the meeting. As the staff and rules within the rehab changed, so did the tone of the meeting.

A few years in a row, in excess of $1,000 was spent on the group's anniversary party. The monies collected in the Seventh Tradition basket came from outside AAs, rehab clients, and family members. What about being "fully self-supporting"?

There was a voice of light through all this darkness. The group was listed with the General Service Office and had a GSR (general service representative) who patiently and consistently suggested that things were not quite right. His was a minority voice, constantly ignored, but he never gave up.

Nor did my sponsor, who guided me into general service work at a very early point in my sobriety. In the end, those few of us left held a group conscience meeting and agreed that this was not, in fact, an autonomous AA group. Eight years after its start, we voted to dissolve the group. A number of changes at the facility itself also contributed to the decision, but the key issue was that this group, with the best of intentions, was not founded on or guided by AA's Traditions.

Carrying the message into treatment facilities works best when AA members take meetings into facilities, rather than forming home groups in facilities. The suggestion that groups no longer call facilities "home" is a positive step toward underlining and strengthening AA's Tradition of cooperation without affiliation. Over the years, treatment facilities committees have developed guidelines, support materials, and a wealth of experience. Let's relearn how to bridge the gap between AA and treatment facilities while remaining within our Traditions.

Annemarie M.
Brockton, Massachusetts

The Only Help We Have to Offer
May 1990

I drank for a long time and couldn't stop. I tried everything. One day, in the midst of planning to take a trip, I called AA. I told the woman who answered the phone that I was an alcoholic going on a trip and I needed a ride. I was afraid to drive to the bus station because I was too drunk, and I couldn't call my parents because they were mad at me about my drinking. The woman told me politely that AA wasn't a taxi service and to call back when I wanted to stop drinking.

I did call back and two wonderful women came to my house. They said and did all the right things and I found myself at my first meeting. At meetings, I began to hear the message of recovery. But I became distracted when I noticed the abundance of single men at every meeting. This must be the answer, I thought. I'll find a man to take care of me. So I pursued that avenue of "recovery" for a time until I became convinced that it wasn't working. Again I returned to AA, this time to listen to the real message of recovery. And I heard it.

Without exception, everyone who had anything I wanted talked about having developed a relationship with a power greater than himself as the result of taking the Twelve Steps. The Big Book quotes Dr. Silkworth as saying, "The message which can interest and hold these alcoholic people must have depth and weight." That's what recovery through the Twelve Steps had for me.

I needed a job. I told people at meetings that it would be easier for me to stay sober if I had a job (and a husband and some friends). They told me that my job was to stay sober. God would take care of the other things when I was ready.

I found a home group because somebody told me I should. I was there at the once-a-week meeting. Soon I discovered that the members met other days at each other's homes and sometimes went places together. I thought this might be the social life that had long eluded me. What a surprise to find out that these gatherings in their homes were group business meetings and studies of the Traditions. Their excursions were visits to small AA groups in outlying communities where they shared their experience, strength, and hope. When they went out for coffee or meals after meetings, the primary topic of discussion was Alcoholics Anonymous. Recovery, unity, service, and the Twelve Steps seemed to intrude into everything we did together! I ended up learning many valuable social skills by hanging around with these people, but social growth was never our purpose in getting together.

When my home group elected me to represent them at the local central committee, I learned about another part of our Fellowship. This committee, in addition to providing a twenty-four-hour answering service, meeting directories, public information, and a forum for discussion of group problems, had a social committee with its own bank account and fun-filled calendar. But to my surprise, as social as their activities were, they always featured AA meetings and speakers, and whether decorating a hall, mopping a floor, or carving a turkey, they always talked about recovery through the Twelve Steps and carrying the AA message to the alcoholic who suffered among us or who hadn't found us yet.

The man who encouraged my participation in general service tried to attract me by describing the wonderful assemblies I'd attend out of town and all the new friends I'd make. He was right, but once again I found that what held us together at those assemblies was our focus on service to Alcoholics Anonymous and how to better carry the AA message to the still suffering alcoholic.

One day while taking calls for our local AA answering service, I got a call from a woman who wanted someone from AA to come see her drunken neighbor who hadn't cleaned her house in ages. "You've got to get someone out here to clean up her house. Don't you people try to help drunks?" I was reminded of my first call to AA looking for a taxi service. Now I know through experience that we're not simply here to "help." The primary purpose of an AA group is to carry the AA message of recovery to the alcoholic who still suffers. The only help we have to offer is the AA program of recovery. We don't offer taxi service, housekeeping, assertiveness training, marriage counseling, jobs, money, mates, or any of the dozens of other services and solutions that each of us thought would solve our problems.

If Alcoholics Anonymous had provided me with a social life, a job, and a husband, I'd have had no reason to place my reliance upon God. If they had done anything other than carry the message of recovery, I might have missed it. Thank God that's all AA does.

Each of us, having had a spiritual awakening as the result of the Twelve Steps, tries to carry this message to the alcoholic who wants it. This is how I stay sober. And if you keep coming back, you don't have to drink again either, if you don't want to.

B. M.
Eureka, California

AA Needs More Than Just Money

July 1992

On Thursday, December 23, 1982, I walked through the door of my first AA speakers meeting. There in the doorway, behind a small wooden table which held a basket full of money and a roll of tickets, sat an older gray-haired gentleman. This must be where they charge admission, I remember thinking. My whole AA experience at that point was two discussion meetings in the previous twenty-four hours.

After managing to sneak in without paying, I found myself an empty seat and took it feeling both self-satisfied and guilty about my imagined deception. At the break my guilt disappeared and embarrassment took its place when the winning raffle tickets were drawn. The group also passed a basket for voluntary contributions to cover group expenses. I found that the ticket table I had so stealthily bypassed was only selling raffle tickets for AA books; they were not charging admission.

I learned later, after reading a copy of *Dr. Bob and the Good Old-timers* (won in another group raffle), that AA has never charged admission. That book taught me a great deal and inspired me to read AA's other literature and to learn more about our Fellowship's history. Among other things, I learned about the spiritual roots of our Seventh Tradition and discovered that we are self-supporting for two primary reasons.

First, we are self-supporting because we do not understand the principle of freely giving when we are new, and the Seventh Tradition helps to drive home our primary purpose. We can let newcomers know that we do not care whether they contribute financially or not. Most drunks are immediately suspicious of anyone who is trying to "make a buck" at their expense, and through the Seventh Tradition newcomers learn that we are here to stay sober and to help others achieve sobriety. By keeping the profit motive completely out of our dealings with fresh new AAs, we can more easily win their trust.

Second, I learned that by declining outside contributions we prove ourselves respectable to an outside world that has a jaded view of causes which always seem to have their hands out. Our refusal of outside contributions lends credibility to our Fellowship. This refusal also prevents outsiders from controlling our Fellowship by controlling our purse strings.

These philosophical observations about the Seventh Tradition are nice, and it is fascinating to learn how our Traditions have developed, but as with all of AA's program, I need to ask myself, How has this Tradition worked its way into my personal life?

A few years back, when the General Service Conference was discussing the Seventh Tradition, I became aware that perhaps my single dollar in the basket was not enough anymore. Nothing I could purchase for one dollar when I got sober in 1982 can be purchased for a dollar today, so why haven't I increased my contribution? Well, sometimes I have. My home group always gets two dollars now, but I can still be quite tightfisted with my money at other groups I attend. This is especially true when I attend groups which are "not spending their money right." And although this problem is covered in the Sixth Tradition, I am especially critical of groups who contribute group money to non-AA entities such as rest homes.

Of course, you know who is wrongly sitting in judgment when I start criticizing any group but my home group. I need to learn to give freely at all the groups I attend. Even two dollars a night is less than I used to spend on beer. And if I really feel strongly about a group's misuse of AA funds I can try to change that misuse, or I can attend another meeting.

At about one year of sobriety, I was chosen as treasurer of my home group. Shortly afterward we changed meeting halls. The new hall was more expensive and each week we barely squeaked by, some weeks even taking in less money than we spent. I explained the situation to the group and made repeated pleas to "go a little heavier on the hat," but those pleas fell on deaf ears. The group finally moved to a less expensive hall and the problem was solved.

This incident taught me something very important about Tradition Seven. I learned that while many times we need to increase our income, there are also times when we need to take a look at our expenses. We need to ask ourselves, "Where can we cut our expenses without losing our ability to carry the message?" In my home group's case the message was carried just as well in the cheap hall as it was in the expensive one.

In serving our area as DCM (district committee member) and later as area treasurer, I learned another lesson about Tradition Seven: Sometimes group contributions, or the withholding of them, are an expression of the group conscience. I have seen groups and districts, unhappy with the way AA affairs were being handled, which withheld or threatened to withhold contributions. I can think of few more direct or powerful expressions of the group conscience than this. Faced with shortages of funds, AA service entities sit up and take notice.

And what about my time? Isn't a donation of my time and services just as important as my donation of cash? What if my home group had money for coffee, rent, and literature for jail meetings, but no one to take the meetings in? And what about public information, treatment facilities, phone answering, and all the other varieties of Twelfth Step work? These all require more than just money; they require contributions of time and service. I need to be as willing to give my time as I am to give my money, for it seems that when AA service is the most inconvenient I receive the greatest rewards.

Finally, all those years of fiddling with AA finances have taught me something about my own financial affairs. In looking at myself I found that I could easily tell my home group, district, area, and even GSO when their spending was out of line with their income, but I refused to take the same hard look at my own finances. I could speak eloquently about AA's need to be less extravagant and to live within its means, but was I living within my means?

No, in fact, I was not.

This revelation caused me to look more closely at my own financial house and to take steps to put it in order. As always it is easier to take someone else's inventory than to take my own, but when I started to practice the very principles I had been preaching to others, my own finances got miraculously more manageable.

I find that many AAs associate the Seventh Tradition only with contribution baskets. But in studying and trying to practice this Tradition—not only in my AA service, but in my daily life—I have learned lessons in giving which I might never have learned otherwise. And I am sure the learning has only begun.

Kreg K.
Manassas, Virginia

The Beauty of Tradition Ten
July 1991

Sobriety in AA is the first thing in my life that has really worked. I'm grateful to fellow AAs who've shown me how not to drink on a daily basis, and to alcoholics I've never met who established our Steps, Traditions, and Concepts for World Service. When I live these principles to the best of my ability, they keep me sober and in touch with the God of my understanding.

I'm especially grateful for Tradition Ten, where it is suggested that AA groups never get involved in the messy business of debating outside issues. The wonderful "extra" implied by this Tradition is that I, as an individual recovering alcoholic, am free to simply enjoy sobriety in AA, without having to defend my position on any outside issue.

You see, I grew up in the sixties. I lived with my parents (one alcoholic, one social drinker) who were closely associated with a small, left-wing, private college in the Northeast. It was a school where expressing your opinions in public was very important. On campus, where I hung out as a thirteen-year-old, I heard lots of angry rhetoric about Vietnam, civil rights, and a lot else. My parents brought the same kind of political anger home with them, and challenged me to come up with informed positions on the same issues. I was only an eighth grader, but I was expected to engage in adult-style discussions. If I didn't have an opinion on the issue at hand, I was considered a failure or a nonthinker.

Looking back, it was probably great training for a future alcoholic. I got very good at hiding the things I was truly ashamed of (especially the amount I drank), using a smoke screen of vaguely directed political opinion.

As my disease progressed, I was often broke, unemployed, hungover, and in need of a place to stay. Usually, my parents would take me in, and for months at a time I'd live at home, trying to get my act together. Deep down inside I knew I was sick and crazy from booze. But at the time, dealing with it was too frightening. It was easier to engage my parents in a petty debate over some global issue beyond our control than to draw attention to the real reason I was out of work.

Today, I'm sober and grateful for what it was like, what happened, and what it's like now. I'm even grateful to my parents, who put up with me as an active alcoholic while also living with their own illnesses. But I'm especially grateful to the alcoholics who founded this Fellowship and gave us the guidelines by which we run our groups. Tradition Ten frees AAs to concentrate on what we have in common—recovery, unity, service—rather than waste time debating outside issues. Angry debate of things over which we have no power can only serve to split us.

Matt F.
Brooklyn, New York

We've Made a Decision—Don't Confuse Us with the Facts!
February 1985

I hate speakers who begin their talks with a definition, because I feel I must be an idiot if they have to define a word for me. However, the Random House College Dictionary defines the word "inform" as follows: "to train or instruct; to supply knowledge or enlightenment." The opposite of inform is conceal.

It is probably close to the truth to say that most AA problems come right back to the *un*informed group conscience. For instance: not supporting district, area, or GSO; not participating in district or area affairs; having group bosses instead of group servants; not permitting God to express himself in our group conscience, by failing to have a group conscience meeting.

Painful as it may be, the place to start in achieving an informed group conscience is with myself. I remember when I was new and judgmental. I told an old-timer that the group was crazy—and he told me to go over in the corner and count myself. That has not always been an easy task for me. My first sponsor took me to a group conscience meeting in my home group and later to district and area meetings, where I found the group conscience again at work. He introduced me to our AA literature, especially *AA Comes of Age*, as well as our AA guidelines and *The AA Service Manual*.

So through the years, it has been the sum total of all my AA experiences that I take with me to the group conscience meeting. And still I find my home group voting to do the exact opposite of what I talked them into last month. We have a little sign hanging on the wall of our meeting room that fits me pretty well. It says: "It is what you learn after you know it all that counts." I suspect that this process of becoming informed may be never-ending.

I believe that for a group conscience to be well informed, we must become knowledgeable about many things. First, we must be knowledgeable about our Twelve Traditions. The future of our entire Fellowship depends on it. All we have to do is look back to the first half of the last century to see what happened to the Washingtonians. It's no exaggeration to say that the Washingtonian Society might be flourishing today had it had our Traditions.

Second, for the group conscience to be informed, someone in the group had better know something about service and our service structure. How often we have heard a member, not necessarily a new member, dismiss service with the comment "That's all politics—let's talk about recovery." I wonder how we could talk about recovery if there hadn't been service first. If there hadn't been service, how would that newcomer ever have heard about AA? I've been raised in AA to believe that service is giving it away in order to keep it. I don't know how to separate service from recovery. As one old-timer said, "Before, we were irresponsible; now, we try to be responsible."

I'm not sure that it's possible for a group to isolate itself totally from AA as a whole, not if that group buys AA literature from the General Service Office. But the uninvolved group can get every bit as sick as the individual member who says, "To hell with the group." A group that doesn't become a part of district or area affairs is practicing a very dangerous game of bigshotism. It is saying in effect, "We don't need those guys." It is like me as a newcomer, saying that the group was crazy and I knew best. This kind of reasoning results in the group's failing to exercise any responsibility in carrying the AA message into prisons or taking action to help get the AA message into the home of the drunk who lives only five blocks from the meeting place. I firmly believe that such groups deny true spiritual recovery to their own members. For unity, the need to be an active part of a larger, broader perspective, is directly opposed to the sick and lonely self-centeredness that was my drinking life.

I want to share with you an example of what can be achieved by ensuring that the group conscience is informed. Two years ago in

New Mexico, only slightly more than half of our groups contributed to GSO. In late 1982, I talked it over with my sponsor, a past delegate, and wrote a letter to each group that hadn't contributed. The letter was intended to clear up a lack of understanding about why we need to contribute to GSO. The price of literature, it explained, is set to meet the costs of services that we demand from GSO—those expenses not met through group contributions. So even if a group contributes to GSO, it must pay higher literature prices because of groups that do not contribute.

The results of this letter were amazing. By the end of 1982, 72.9% of our groups in New Mexico had contributed to GSO. That ended up being the fifth highest percentage among the seventy-six delegate areas in the United States. It all seems to come down to being able to explain why.

Then, I wonder how often we go on to share our experiences with newcomers regarding the Higher Power—God as we understand him, as he has chosen to express himself in our group conscience. In the group I belong to, the blindest of us can look back over the past years and see the hand of a Higher Power in our group conscience decisions. How often in AA elections has a name been pulled from the hat when we couldn't get the two-thirds majority necessary in balloting, and later on it is clear that there could not have been any other choice. To me, this is a perfect illustration of doing our part and letting God do his.

I have learned, too, that I can be bad for my group. I can pursue my own egotistical needs, or I can give myself over to the group with a willingness to serve. But a group can be bad for me, too. A sponsor once told me, "If your group allows you to be a big shot, it is the wrong group for you." He was exactly right.

In summary, if we are to truly achieve an informed group conscience, we will as individuals ensure that we are knowledgeable about our AA way of life. We will read our literature and be willing to share that with newcomers. We will understand and participate in our service structure. We will ensure that we truly have group conscience meetings. Dealing with the group conscience has always involved, for me, reliance on the Serenity Prayer. The elements of serenity, courage, and wisdom have been essential. However, it is a tremendous comfort to me to know that our Higher Power, God as I choose to call him, does express himself in our group conscience.

I want AA to survive for myself, for my son, and for the as yet unborn members of the future. And that requires that I become responsible. God will indeed take care of us, but only if we do our part.

D. L.
Alamogordo, New Mexico

Try It Standing Up
July 2000

'm very protective of my home group for the same reason that most alcoholics are: if the group doesn't survive, neither will I. A couple of months ago at a business meeting, my home group had a heated discussion over whether or not to say the Lord's Prayer at the end of our group's meetings. Saying it certainly seems to contradict AA's claim to have no affiliations with any sect or denomination. Furthermore, as a skittish newcomer, I remember being very uncomfortable sitting in a church basement saying a prayer that's a prominent part of Christian liturgy.

But my sponsor said, "Get over it." And I have to admit, it has never hurt me to say a prayer, especially one conceived by a loving teacher, teaching me to praise God's name, to wish for God's will to be done, and to remind myself I will be forgiven only to the degree that I forgive others. The Lord's Prayer certainly feels paternalistic. (So, does that mean we should be saying the Hail Mary instead?) The Serenity Prayer may feel less sectarian, but it stems from religion, too. So in that case, rather than wishing to shut the door on our past, maybe we should acknowledge AA's debt to the Oxford Movement, Reverend Shoemaker, Father Dowling, and Sister Ignatia, just to name a few.

Have I managed to offend you yet? To get your juices going? Because that's what happened at our business meeting. We all got churned up and disagreeable. And afterward, there was a hangover, a lingering air of resentment. Now when we form a circle and join hands at the end of our regular meeting, we all feel the tension. A moment that used to exemplify our unity now underscores our differences.

The idea that issues and resentments generated in a business meeting are spilling over into the "real" meeting troubles me. I suppose without business meetings, resentments might smolder anyway, but I think we fanned the fire. I got the feeling that things were just going too smoothly for us drama-loving alcoholics, so we latched onto something controversial to add a little excitement to the proceedings.

To the extent that we were just "stirring the pot," we were following a longstanding tradition in AA. But not the Traditions of Alcoholics Anonymous. One Tradition calls for us to "practice a genuine humility" and to silence "the clamor of desires and ambitions whenever these could damage the group." For me, that clamor is the need to comment on everything, to throw in my two cents so you'll know just how smart I am. It's the urge to jump in and mix it up as if a business meeting were a barroom brawl. I need to practice some restraint, to emulate the example of the elder statesman in Tradition Two who "is willing to sit quietly on the sidelines patiently awaiting developments."

My friend G. had an interesting suggestion: Why not hold our business meetings standing up? I know I'd pontificate less if I had to stand more. How often have I told myself, If I have to sit through this meeting, then I should at least get to air my point of view, even if it's already been expressed by several others. Maybe our feet are better judges of when we've said enough than our minds.

And if business meetings were shorter and to the point, maybe more people would get involved. Since our group conscience is how the loving God expresses himself to us, the more conscience, the more God, right? Let the primary purpose of a business meeting be to make sure the rent is paid, the key positions are filled, and there's enough literature and sponsorship available to help the newcomer. Keep it simple. Tradition Nine says, "Alcoholics Anonymous needs the least possible organization." Save the controversy for a letter to Grapevine. Our "meeting in print" has shown for over fifty years that it can handle controversy. It even thrives on it.

Of course, I should have a bit more faith in my group's ability to weather contentious business meetings. What doesn't kill us makes us stronger. In which case, I have just made much ado about nothing. I probably should have written this standing up.

J. W.
Maplewood, New Jersey

Enjoying Anonymity
January 1992

I had never been to an AA meeting before, but the counselor had said that it would start at 8 o'clock. It was now 7:55. Other people were going in and walking up the stairs.

Well, I thought, if I didn't like it I could always get up and leave; they can't make me stay. Nobody says I have to go, anyway. Okay. Up the stairs I go.

It's a large room with tables down the center, some theater seats by the windows, a coffee urn in the corner. The whole place smelled of smoke. Not wanting to be obtrusive, I took a seat in the corner.

The person seemingly in charge sat at the head of the table. Behind him hung the portraits of two men. They began in a businesslike manner with a moment of silence followed by a prayer and the reading of several lengthy statements called the Steps and Traditions.

What was said sounded familiar to me, stories and problems that happened to me or to someone I knew. It felt good to be with people who understood the circumstances that I was experiencing. They were open and honest about their troubles and conflicts. Toward the end the guy at the head of the table read a statement about anonymity: "Who you see here, what you hear here, when you leave here, let it stay here."

It would be some time before I would understand the meaning of that phrase. On the one hand it said mind your own business, what a person shares with the group is not to be discussed outside the meeting. If he's having a problem with his boss and I know who the boss is, what was said should remain confidential. It would dawn on me in time that people are relieved of the burdens of guilt, anger, resentment, self-pity and other emotional baggage by speaking out and talking about the things that troubled them so. That was a key to the success of the program. Those who were concerned about how their story sounded to others or who wanted to look better than they were feeling were not making much headway in recovery. They were becoming actors who said what others wanted to hear.

At first I thought everyone was ashamed to be here, because that's how I felt. Soon I recognized an old neighbor of mine, whom I hadn't seen in years. I didn't know whether I should hide from him or walk up and say hello. Later I found that he had several years in the program and he became my first sponsor. It was not apparent to me that admitting that I was alcoholic and accepting it as a fact of life were two very different things. After acceptance, the shame melted into the new interest that I soon took in my recovery, knowing that at last I was working in the right direction. With acceptance of my disease of alcoholism came a full-fledged effort to work all aspects of the recovery program. I began to attend the Step study groups and really put them to practice.

Recovery took on a familiar pattern. The people who were sincere about staying sober showed up regularly for meetings, set up the tables and chairs, got out the books and literature. They were greeting the newcomers and making them feel welcome. They participated when called upon and listened intently while others spoke of their experience. They set an example by helping and lending a hand when needed.

Last names and job titles had nothing to do with recovery. What mattered was what was shared at the table and the conduct in this small room. The ones who beat the drum the loudest are just trying to attract attention to themselves. The ones who have got the serenity do not need to bring attention to themselves, for they are content just being themselves. Humility is a personal achievement, it cannot be given away. It comes in glimmers and grows like an ice crystal. It is fragile, too, thus requiring constant care and protection.

Maintaining anonymity insures that the focus of our efforts is on the program and not the personalities.

Fred E.
Seattle, Washington

My Vote: No Opinion
October 2016

When I was in very early sobriety, a woman who always had an amazing way of sharing attended my home group. She was funny, sharp and always seemed to say something I identified with and needed to hear. It was as if my Higher Power cleverly had her say words just for me.

At that time, the country was heavily focused on a presidential election. News organizations covered it nonstop. Many of my conversations with my family centered on the presidential debates and the candidates. The election was almost impossible to avoid.

During one of our home group meetings one day, the woman I so dearly loved to listen to spoke up. She talked about one of the two candidates and that candidate's political party. It just so happened that I supported the opposing party. Not only did I not agree with her point of view, but I felt offended by her words.

I didn't speak at that meeting but later I told my sponsor about what had happened. We had a lovely discussion about acceptance and the Tenth Tradition. I felt that if this woman had truly understood the full scope of Tradition Ten and the impact of her words, she would have spoken differently.

Now when she shared, I found flaws in everything she said. I even hoped that at meetings she wouldn't be called on to speak. I no longer heard any message of recovery in her words.

My sobriety has progressed over the years. I don't put as much stock in what other people say in meetings about their personal beliefs. I can easily discard words I don't agree with or dislike. We all can learn from the example of the many once hugely successful Washingtonians, whose demise strongly influenced our Tenth Tradition.

As with everything I find offensive, I need to look at myself and see what I can learn from the experience of feeling offended. I take special care not to voice my political opinions or my view on other controversial topics at meetings or with my sponsees. Recently I asked one of my long-time sponsees if she knew which political party I support, now that we're barreling into another presidential election that will undoubtedly be contentious.

She said she had no clue. That's exactly the response I wanted to hear. I still look forward to hearty political discussions with my family but I don't ever want anyone in the rooms, especially newcomers, to think that what I say in meetings and my sobriety are flawed based on my personal opinions on outside issues.

Jenine M.
Atlanta, Georgia

Our Primary Purpose
May 2021

I love my home group. I'm not trying to say it's the best in the world, because my hope is that everyone feels that way about their own home group. But for me, ours is the best.

Our group started in 1998, and our name is Primary Purpose. I feel it truly depicts us and what we are about. Tradition Five long form reminds me that "each Alcoholics Anonymous group ought to be a spiritual entity..." and I truly feel we are.

I arrive at my home group an hour before the meeting starts. The room has already been set up and the crew has gone to dinner. There's usually about five or so minutes when I'm there by myself, and I sit and feel the spirit before the "entity" starts and our members begin to trickle in. That's when the place comes alive. I listen to the glad tidings and the laughter. I can smell the coffee. I see the smiles of the regulars and the scared faces of our new friends as they enter.

Tradition Five goes on to say, "Each group has but one primary purpose—to carry its message to the alcoholic who still suffers." What is my group's message? I know what my message is, but my group's?

Well the first thing is...our group is accessible for members using wheelchairs. We post signs so people will know where we're located. We have at least two greeters at our door to welcome people. We have a nice literature area, which includes Grapevine and La Viña and other AA literature. We also have CDs of past speakers and birthday cards for members to sign. We also have a table with AA pamphlets and flyers of upcoming events. At the front of the room are the three window shades: Steps, Traditions and Concepts. We have lots of coffee and donuts, plenty of comfy seats and a spirit in the room that's alive.

If you happen to sit down before our meeting starts, be advised you will continually be approached and welcomed. You might even be invited to meet others.

The meeting starts promptly at 8 P.M. and we all take our seats. We appreciate the quiet respect shown during the readings and our speakers.

During our announcements you'll hear how to get involved with Hospitals & Institutions service. We offer help with getting a sponsor, literature or service commitments. We also announce annual AA birthdays, as well as reports on Grapevine, La Viña, General Service and intergroup. We wrap up at 9:15 with a prayer. Fellowship continues until around 10. Our group's message is one of recovery, unity and service in action. I think I'll keep coming back.

Try this: The next time you visit your home group, pretend you're a newcomer or a visitor. Ask yourself...what do you see, feel, hear? Is your group contributing to that spiritual entity? It's a lifeline for many. May that lifeline be strong.

Debbie D.
Concord, California

SECTION FIVE

Using Technology

My Friends in the Outback
September 2021

My husband has 39 years of sobriety and I have 31. We had established our "nonnegotiable" Friday date nights about the same time I started attending virtual meetings in Alice Springs, Australia. Little did I know, when I first pushed the "join" button to the Alice Springs meetings, how my life would be forever changed and enriched by a group so far away.

My husband and I live in Alexandria, Virginia. During the pandemic, I had to learn new technology skills to attend online AA meetings. I had just barely learned how to text my grandchildren on my smartphone and now I had to learn how to log onto meetings on my computer pad.

Once I became comfortable with daily meetings, I began to explore AA meetings in different states and then, to my surprise, meetings in other countries! I was intrigued by a small women's meeting I found in Australia on Saturday mornings. Due to time zone differences, I had to log in on Friday nights to attend.

At first, my husband and I continued our date nights by starting out for the restaurant a little earlier. I would have my dessert wrapped and ready to go home for the meeting. Eventually, we decided that this meeting was more important than our date nights.

Once I clicked on the meeting link to Alice Springs, I noticed the Steps and Traditions were posted on the wall. The meeting was not in somebody's house, but in a conference room in a hospital. I started to relax when I heard the familiar words of the Preamble and "How It Works," even if some of the words were pronounced a little funny. I knew I was home.

Each week, the ladies of Alice Springs welcomed me, and slowly I assimilated to a different way of stating my sobriety date and a few slang words and phrases. I soon realized that the AA message is the same in Alice Springs as it is in Alexandria or, for that matter, Cleveland or San Francisco.

As we shared our common experiences in our struggles to stay sober, other ladies joined us and got caught up in our eagerness to help the newcomer get sober. I admit I was slightly jealous when the Aussies could share phone numbers and I couldn't. Long distance phone calls, especially overseas calls, would put a crimp in our budget.

That problem changed when I became friends with several of the ladies in the group on social media. I will never forget my first international phone call through my computer. I even switched over to "video chats."

At first I was apprehensive about what these chats would do to our monthly phone bill, but I soon realized that our phone and internet were two separate bills and now I am free to talk with anybody in another country without worrying about the cost. That rocketed me into another dimension alright. And getting acquainted with the gorgeous landscape of Australia and its animals through my new friends was frosting on the cupcake of fellowship.

But the most influential experience of my sobriety, besides doing my Fourth and Fifth Steps, was attending the virtual 55th Australian National Convention in Toowoomba, Queensland, that October. A buddy from Alice Springs and I wondered why we had to pay $100 for a virtual convention when there really shouldn't be any expense, and I must admit that I had very low expectations. Most of my experiences at conventions had involved meeting people in person and I didn't have any idea how I would meet anybody there virtually. Boy was I wrong!

I committed myself to getting all I could out of my $100 investment. I went so far as to move into the guest room of our apartment with the intention of living on Australian time during the conference. I slept during the day and went to meetings during the early mornings. I even walked my dogs on Australian time!

I was pleased to find that the conference was well-organized. There were preconvention videos, as well as opportunities to set up a personal profile complete with video, biographical sketch and contact information. I did have a little trouble remembering the password "Toowoomba," as I kept changing the letters to Wootoomba. With a little practice, the spelling became second nature to me.

I was impressed with the convention from beginning to end. The organization and planning were phenomenal. Talks by Alateens, Al-Anons and AA members were inspiring. There was even a virtual play, a drama featuring the characters of Bill and Lois. We played a game called "Kahoot!" that tested knowledge of the Australian history of AA, and it kept my head spinning. I was so glad that I had the foresight to bring a notebook to take notes. I loved the virtual tour of Toowoomba. I felt like I was on a tour bus with all of my Aussies, driving on the wrong side of the road.

One of the best experiences was hearing a talk given by a Jesuit from New York named Father Bill. He told the tale of the early history of AA and the Oxford Group. He summarized the Twelve Steps and ended with the moving prayer that has had a deep impact on my spiritual life. Something changed inside of me as I heard the "Step Aside" prayer for the first time. Now I say it weekly with a prayer buddy.

When the conference souvenir book arrived in the mail, I was blown away by the history of how AA came to Australia. But I never got past a superficial thumbing of the book because of an insert that fell out of it. It was the recipe for Lamington cake, which I had heard so much about.

I immediately set out on a mission to assemble the ingredients and my husband and I made the cake. But there was one problem I didn't see beforehand: the metric system! Now I had to learn the temperature of the oven and how much butter to put in. Our cake didn't turn out like the one in the photo however, and if I ever get to Australia, that cake is one of the first things I will order.

It may seem hard to believe, but I now consider Alice Springs to be my new home group, even though it's on the other side of the world. With the close-knit fellowship of such a small group, we have gotten to know each other on a very personal level.

I have even been able to provide service to the group as host and cohost. I practice the Seventh Tradition by contributing to the GSO in the name of the Darwin district, and we all carry the AA message to fellow alcoholics the world over.

Terrie S.
Alexandria, Virginia

Making Lemonade
December 2021

One morning, at the very beginning of the COVID-19 pandemic, about four of us were in our virtual AA meeting. We were laughing and enjoying just seeing one another, even if it was in little "Brady Bunch" squares on a screen, which was super new to us at the time. All of a sudden this fellow clicked into the meeting. He was sipping a beer! It was only 7 A.M.

Our conversation shifted naturally to welcoming him. He told us his name was Mark and he couldn't stop drinking, and that if he didn't stop he felt he was going to die. He said he needed help. He was very emotional.

I will never forget the power of the next few moments. My friends, my AA family, this group I'm so proud to be a part of, snapped into Twelfth Step mode. We shifted the topic to Step One and we all shared about how we got sober. We even told our own experiences with morning drinking. We laughed about it but also wove in the seriousness of this disease. Mark visibly relaxed.

As I was sharing, Mark paused his video, went to the fridge and we heard him crack another beer. We forged on. This is not something that would ever happen in a live meeting but here we were. Phillip, one of our members, asked Mark to get something to write with and gave him his phone number. Phillip told him to call. Mark said he would. And he did.

Mark kept coming every morning for weeks. We referred to him as our "zoom baby." We never judged him or made him feel unwelcome. He kept thanking us over and over. This went on for a month, maybe two. One of our regulars, J.T., asked him for his address, then took a Big Book and placed it in Mark's mailbox. J.T. keeps Big Books in his trunk for just this purpose. Mark was in shock that someone would care enough to do such a thing. He talked about opening that mailbox and finding J.T.'s Big Book for weeks.

We all prayed for Mark every day. Since he was still drinking, we offered him assistance with finding a hospital or rehab. Finally Mark surrendered, went to a hospital and stopped drinking. Mark now is a member of the Happy Hour AA group in nearby Killen. He has a very different life now with his wife and family, and the members here at our 4-D virtual meeting witnessed the entire process. It's something I will remember for the rest of my life. As my sponsor loves to quote, "It works, it really does."

Recently Mark said to me, "Thank goodness I found you guys on my computer or I would be dead by now! I'm so thankful y'all accepted me as I was!"

For me, these virtual meetings have opened my world in an amazing way. I lived in Paris for almost two decades and in New York for almost 10 years. I have logged into meetings in both Paris and New York and reunited with friends I haven't seen since we got sober together more than 25 years ago. I'm even cochairing a virtual meeting in New York City this term right here from Alabama! My fellow cochair, who also got sober in New York, is in Chicago now. Worlds are coming together and enriching sobriety for so many of us—including me. I've heard newcomers say they just keep these online meetings running all day and night on their phones. They say it gives them comfort to know that we're always there.

One morning we had two women show up and share that they were zooming through 50 states in 50 days. They had knocked several states off their list and found our meeting when searching "Alabama AA meetings." I love all this action AA members have taken during the pandemic. We're making lemonade out of lemons!

Elizabeth R.
Florence, Alabama

The Meeting Goes On
May 2019

I hate to miss my Saturday morning meeting. It's my home group and I've been attending it for the last 15 years. I never miss this meeting unless I am deathly ill or if there's a major, dangerous storm going on.

One time a blizzard started at about 10:00 the night before our meeting, and by the time I woke up there was already a few inches of the white stuff on the ground. The wind was so strong it was blowing the snow horizontally. The predictions that morning were for an unprecedented couple of feet of snow over the next few hours. The weather people were telling everyone to stay indoors where it was safe. The roads were already slippery and dangerous. So no meeting for me that day.

A friend from our group messaged a few of us on social media, asking if anyone was going to the meeting. Someone who lived close by was going to show up at the venue just in case some cold soul went to any lengths to get to a meeting. I was glad we were "covered," so if someone came by the hand of AA would be there.

But why should the rest of us miss out if we could "meet" on our private web group? It was a safe place there. The rest of the world couldn't see what we posted. The friend invited everyone he could think of from his other meetings to join us in a conversation and I did the same, including some sober friends from other states.

By 10:30 A.M., our usual meeting time, we had assembled about a dozen sober people from all over in our little messenger "room." I typed out the Serenity Prayer to get us started. My friend introduced a topic and we started our virtual meeting.

OK, it was a little chaotic. Folks were not very quick to respond. Some didn't take it seriously (you know how alcoholics are!). But there were some good insights that started to be shared from the sober friends we had gathered. Sometimes comments were jumbled together as we all "spoke" at once. One woman shared a photo of her dog in the snow. There were "thumbs up" and cartoon emojis instead of, "Thanks for sharing." But it was a real AA meeting that we couldn't have attended otherwise.

Bill and Bob could not have conceived of an AA meeting ever occurring the way the one that Saturday morning did. But we stayed sober that day in the midst of a record-making blizzard. We reached out to each other and we were there for each other. We weren't going to let a few snowflakes stop us.

Judith H.
Morristown, New Jersey

800 Miles Away
December 2021

I currently live in a North Dakota town of 200 people. The closest meeting is 50 miles away and is held at 8:00 P.M. To travel at night is no longer an option for me.

After more than three years of being unable to attend meetings and with very limited contact with AA, I drank again. The law placed me into a medical treatment center. At that time, I had been drinking for two months and the progression of my disease was astronomical.

I originally sobered up in AA at age 15 in August of 1980. Many years later, after picking up my 21-year chip, I also picked up a drink. After that, I would sober up for a year or so before I drank again. Twice, I stayed sober for seven years. Every time I went back out again to drink, I became involved with the wrong side of the law.

Back in 1981, I had been a founding member of an AA group in a small town in Colorado, the Laporte 287 group. For years, this was my home group. It has always been a smaller meeting, averaging about 12 or 13 folks. The group has two candlelight meetings a week and six open meetings total. The group also actively involves itself in service work.

Today, it has been more than three months since I was discharged from treatment here in North Dakota. I was terrified, sick, alone and desperate the day I was released. I called my old sponsor from the Laporte 287 group back in Colorado. I also called another member from there. She was homebound due to hip surgeries. The group was bringing a meeting into her home once a week. I wanted to be a part of the group again so desperately, but I now lived 800 miles away. At first, I thought there was no way I could participate. Then, while on the phone with her I had an idea. Maybe I could "attend" the meeting at her home while on speakerphone, which is one of the few features on my smartphone that I understand how to work.

We tried it and it went well. I soon discovered the conference call feature and tried calling my sponsor while I was on the phone with my homebound friend. It worked! The meeting at her home was small and all the members either knew me or knew of me. The group and my sponsor agreed that I could attend conference call meetings at both locations—the home group meeting and the meeting at my friend's house.

Now I regularly "pick up" my homebound friend on her phone and we go to the Laporte 287 meeting together by phone. My sponsor is our host on her phone. Other members support this arrangement and are very inclusive and encouraging. I always look forward to the five minutes of catching up before and after our meetings.

This phone connection allowed me to attend the group conscience meeting and a three-hour group inventory. I also attend the meetings of a Big Book study group and Traditions study group. And that's not all. Every Saturday night I join the candlelight Grapevine meeting and I get to have daily contact with my sponsor.

My Higher Power has made this all come about in spite of my doubts and my geographical isolation. Today, one of the most basic tools in my spiritual tool kit is my phone. Life has not been this good for me in years.

Barbara B.
Binford, North Dakota

Connected
March 2017

Three years ago, I made a major life change when I again relocated to another state in sobriety. Although it was a good move, and one filled with hope, it meant leaving another AA family behind.

I had lived with that sober community in the far suburbs of Chicago for 20 years. I was going to miss them terribly. Twenty years gives a guy quite a while to dig a rut in AA.

Before I bought a new home and moved to northern Michigan, I spent a week in the area to make sure AA was alive and well there. I needed to know that I would find the same support there that I was accustomed to. My only concern about the move was leaving my gay home group for a very remote and rather conservative area. The closest gay meeting to my new home was more than two hours away.

I had been my home group's contact person for the hosting church during my time there. I felt sad when I told the church secretary that I was leaving. I joked that since the closest gay meeting was so far away from my new place, I wished they had better cell phone reception in their church basement so someone could Skype me into the meeting.

A few days later, the church contacted me. I was told the church members had discussed the situation and had decided that they would drop an internet line into the basement's meeting room if I were serious about wanting to stay in contact with the group.

Our group had a few discussions about the issue and we decided to give the technology a try. A few weeks later, they dropped the line into the meeting room and, thanks to a cheap laptop, we were ready to make our attempt at an AA meeting in the age of the internet.

After a few weeks of working out the snags, we were soon up and running. At my old group, that cheap laptop took my place in my usual chair. I was able to resume participation at my home group from two states away!

Some people have commented that they don't think a meeting on a computer screen would be the same as an in-person meeting, or that maybe it wouldn't mean as much. Perhaps that would be the case if I were a stranger to the group. But these are folks I have been meeting with for a very long time. Although AA is very strong up here in the hinterlands of northern Michigan, the computer link helped me to connect with fellow sober LGBT members.

As some of you may have heard from AA members after traveling abroad, sometimes just sitting in an AA meeting helps, even if you don't understand a word of the language being spoken. That has turned out to be the case with the Skyped-in meeting. One evening the microphone on the laptop was out of service. But just watching the members' mouths move in silence while they sat in the same meeting room brought me that sense of ease and comfort.

I'm not the only member to enjoy the ability to connect remotely. There have been a few bonuses we Skype-users have found along the way. When one of the group's regular members is out of town, they don't need to miss the meeting. This has turned out to be quite a blessing for members who are called out of town to deal with family issues, business trips, conventions and vacations, or for members who are simply stuck at home with the flu. It is a comfort to all our group's members to know that even if they are out of town, the support of the program at their home group is just a mouse-click away.

We have heard questions of anonymity raised. First and foremost, it is something that is open only to our members, not a publicly broadcast event for anyone to join. If one of us is connecting via a smartphone from a coffee shop, we sit with our back to the wall so other people don't see the screen. We use headphones and a Bluetooth. If we're connecting while traveling and staying at another person's home, we close the door. It's really not a breach of anonymity if no one else can see or hear what happens at the meeting.

Does making that long-distance connection make a difference? You bet it does. There are times when I have heard exactly what I needed to hear when attending via video connection. As much as I love and respect my local AA people up here, and as much as they support and respect me, there are times when my fellow gay and sober folks are exactly what I need. To continue to share sobriety with my fellow LGBT home group members, with whom I have shared so much sober history, has been a blessing.

Sometimes it's a comfort just seeing the same ugly green walls of the same old meeting room with the broken futon in the corner. Ah, if I close my eyes, I can sometimes still smell the mustiness of the basement!

I understand there are many groups that may be uncomfortable accepting technology into their meeting space like this. That's why we have the group conscience. I can speak on behalf of myself and my home group and say it has been a gift for us all to be able to stay connected when we are far away.

It has been a remarkable journey with my home group for the past three years. With their continued sober support and the new AA family I have made up here, I have the best of both worlds.

Mark H.
Lincoln, Michigan

Zooming Into the Fourth Dimension
August 2020

My husband Steve and I boarded a cruise ship on March 7, just as the COVID-19 virus was beginning to appear in the U.S. Probably ill-advised, we brazenly forged ahead, armed with disinfectant wipes and magical thinking. Any enjoyment we may have anticipated was marred by occasional news updates from home about the frenzied run on paper products and grim reports of an overwhelmed healthcare system. We erred on the side of caution and curtailed our activities about the ship and stayed close to our cabin. Whenever we pulled into a U.S. territory port-of-call, I could collect text updates from my sponsor, Brigitte, and sometimes even make phone calls.

Each day on the cruise I attended a meeting of "Friends of Bill W." on the ship, which welcomed folks in all manner and shape of recovery. Some days as many as 15 AA members were in attendance, which is an impressive number on a cruise. I had met many of these people the previous year on the same charter. As the cruise week wore on, we grew closer and leaned into recovery as the news of home grew more and more grim. We promised to stay in touch. A college professor among us said that once we all returned home, she'd host us for AA meetings on a handy app she uses for teaching. That was the first I heard of virtual meetings.

A week later, on March 14, our cruise ended and we disembarked. At last back on the American shore, though not quite the same one from which we had sailed the week before. Aside from the sudden global addiction to hand sanitizer and toilet paper, the COVID-19 crisis would also create the need to learn new phrases like "social distancing" and "flattening the curve." I wondered aloud about my home group, New Market Tuesday Night.

Once home, I was astonished and gratified to find in my email inbox some information about my home group and how we might continue to meet each week despite our state's stay-at-home order. I just knew they would have this crisis in hand, and true to form, New Market Tuesday Night didn't miss a beat. Contained in the email were instructions on how to access our new virtual meeting and a smattering of information about other online AA meetings starting up immediately—immediately! We held a group conscience meeting right away and added a Big Book study to our home group. "We will intuitively know how to handle situations..." that have never baffled us before and they're not going to baffle us now. Into action!

The stay-at-home order has been a mixed bag for this alcoholic. Telling the likes of me that I must stay home, not go anywhere and see no one was sweet permission to isolate. I even allowed myself to bask in the notion of solitary confinement—briefly. But I've been able to adjust accordingly. Needing mere minutes to prepare to attend my AA meetings from home has been a revelation: quick comb, lovely blouse, ratty sweatpants. Check!

Save for a few interruptions in our internet service, our local AA "zooms" forward. We have no dues or fees, but our Seventh Tradition contributions are made by way of convenient apps. I have not always adjusted well to the shift in communication and commerce wrought by technology. I'm almost 60 (never mind how close) and predictably, I'm resistant. Despite my reluctance to change, I am equal to the task and I'm grateful for the ready solutions and swift action all around us when we all pull together.

Luckily, AA continues to keep me focused..."happiness, peace and usefulness, in a way of life that is incredibly more wonderful as time passes." AA, and specifically the New Market Tuesday Night group and my network of folks in recovery, have helped me find the joy in this new way of life.

Stay safe, stay healthy, and if you're able, stay home.

Scottie B.
New Market, Maryland

The Day I Unmuted
October 2022

I came to AA unsure that I wanted to stop drinking. I had been given an ultimatum by my partner of 15 years: "Choose me or the bottle," she said.

I didn't want to lose my relationship, but I didn't know how to stop drinking. I knew about AA by way of my experience with Al-Anon 25 years earlier. But I didn't think I had a problem with alcohol—it was my father who was the alcoholic, not me. I was just a heavy drinker, not an alcoholic.

And so I came to AA because of my partner. I later learned that it didn't matter which door I went through to get to AA, the important thing was that I opened the door to the possibility of sobriety, even if it was only a crack.

For me, the virtual door of AA online welcomed me with open arms. My recovery hasn't been a smooth journey. I bounced along my bottom prior to establishing the continuous sobriety I enjoy today. Two days without alcohol here, 10 days there. I found it nearly impossible to stop drinking.

Anything could set me off on a bender: an argument, loneliness, boredom. Even excitement and joy caused me to drink. These were all excuses and deep down inside I knew this, but I was unable to be rigorously honest with myself. It's easier to lie than to tell the truth, and each lie brought me back to the bottle.

Although I kept drinking, I learned early on to keep coming back to AA no matter what. And something kept bringing me back, every day. I still find it unbelievable that I attended my online meetings drunk. I didn't participate but I did listen, and eventually people's stories started to sink in and make sense. I started to connect with people's experience, strength and hope. But I couldn't put down those bottles of wine and beer. That is, I couldn't until I found my home group in Lakewood, Ohio.

I live in Canada but where you live doesn't really matter much for an online meeting. That's the beauty of online meetings—you can visit anywhere in the world and feel at home. The Lakewood Freethinkers AA group meets every day at noon and 9:00 P.M. EST. Our group welcomes newcomers and invites anyone to stay for as long as they like without participating. I was amazed that people in the meeting were just glad I was there. I would attend all the meetings anonymously—with my video off and my microphone on mute.

But I listened intently. And then came the day when I unmuted myself and shared for the first time. I shared that I was drinking before meetings. I don't know what came over me, but for the first time I admitted I was a drunk and tears streamed down my face. What relief I felt. The truth. Finally. I had spoke the truth and no one judged me. In fact, a few folks said, "Keep coming back, Tracy."

And that's what I did. I drank and I came back, numerous times. Until one day a member from Lakewood asked me if I wanted to chair the Thursday noon meeting. I quickly said no. I could barely string together four days in a row, so how could I chair? Another member said, "We don't have a minimum sobriety rule. As long as you're sober the day you chair, you can chair."

I was on medical leave from work for post-traumatic stress disorder and had a lot of free time. And I was bored. So, I thought, Why not? I used to facilitate seminar groups in university when I was a doctoral student many years ago so I thought I would try chairing the online AA meeting. I ended up loving it.

And that's how it all started for me—my journey to sobriety. I did drink the day before or the day after I chaired, and I would share in meetings that I was hungover, but I was firmly committed to never drinking on the day that I chaired. I began to chair twice a week, so I'd be sober at least those two days. And then I'd do the readings for a meeting and stay sober that day. And then I'd open the "doors" of the online meeting and stay sober that day. Soon I started to string together two, three, four days in a row and now I have almost eight months of continuous sobriety.

I know that service work has definitely been the key to keeping me sober, not to mention my home group, which I call my Higher Power. I have a sponsor, I do the Steps, I attend and chair a lot of virtual meetings. I feel gratitude and love for the Fellowship and for my home group, which gave me a chance early on to participate in meetings and to feel a part of something larger than myself. And I cherish the latitude extended to me by the group that enabled me to explore and ask questions about AA in a way that resonated and worked for me. That's where I found, as our Big Book says, "a way out on which we can absolutely agree."

Tracy L.
Ottawa, Ontario

The Twelve Steps

1. We admitted we were powerless over alcohol—that our lives had become unmanageable.
2. Came to believe that a Power greater than ourselves could restore us to sanity.
3. Made a decision to turn our will and our lives over to the care of God *as we understood Him.*
4. Made a searching and fearless moral inventory of ourselves.
5. Admitted to God, to ourselves, and to another human being the exact nature of our wrongs.
6. Were entirely ready to have God remove all these defects of character.
7. Humbly asked Him to remove our shortcomings.
8. Made a list of all persons we had harmed, and became willing to make amends to them all.
9. Made direct amends to such people wherever possible, except when to do so would injure them or others.
10. Continued to take personal inventory and when we were wrong promptly admitted it.
11. Sought through prayer and meditation to improve our conscious contact with God *as we understood Him,* praying only for knowledge of His will for us and the power to carry that out.
12. Having had a spiritual awakening as the result of these steps, we tried to carry this message to alcoholics, and to practice these principles in all our affairs.

The Twelve Traditions

1. Our common welfare should come first; personal recovery depends upon A.A. unity.
2. For our group purpose there is but one ultimate authority—a loving God as He may express Himself in our group conscience. Our leaders are but trusted servants; they do not govern.
3. The only requirement for A.A. membership is a desire to stop drinking.
4. Each group should be autonomous except in matters affecting other groups or A.A. as a whole.
5. Each group has but one primary purpose—to carry its message to the alcoholic who still suffers.
6. An A.A. group ought never endorse, finance or lend the A.A. name to any related facility or outside enterprise, lest problems of money, property and prestige divert us from our primary purpose.
7. Every A.A. group ought to be fully self-supporting, declining outside contributions.
8. Alcoholics Anonymous should remain forever nonprofessional, but our service centers may employ special workers.
9. A.A., as such, ought never be organized; but we may create service boards or committees directly responsible to those they serve.
10. Alcoholics Anonymous has no opinion on outside issues; hence the A.A. name ought never be drawn into public controversy.
11. Our public relations policy is based on attraction rather than promotion; we need always maintain personal anonymity at the level of press, radio and films.
12. Anonymity is the spiritual foundation of all our traditions, ever reminding us to place principles before personalities.

AA Grapevine

AA Grapevine is AA's international monthly journal, published continuously since its first issue in June 1944. The AA pamphlet on AA Grapevine describes its scope and purpose this way: "As an integral part of Alcoholics Anonymous since 1944, the Grapevine publishes articles that reflect the full diversity of experience and thought found within the A.A. Fellowship, as does La Viña, the bimonthly Spanish-language magazine, first published in 1996. No one viewpoint or philosophy dominates their pages, and in determining content, the editorial staff relies on the principles of the Twelve Traditions."

In addition to magazines, AA Grapevine, Inc. also produces books, eBooks, audiobooks and other items. It also offers a Grapevine Complete subscription, which includes the print magazine as well as complete online access, with new stories weekly, AudioGrapevine (the audio version of the magazine), the vast Grapevine Story Archive and current online issues of Grapevine and La Viña. Separate ePub versions of the magazines are also available. For more information on AA Grapevine, or to subscribe to any of these, please visit the magazine's website at aagrapevine.org or write to:

AA Grapevine, Inc.
475 Riverside Drive
New York, NY 10115

Alcoholics Anonymous

AA's program of recovery is fully set forth in its basic text, *Alcoholics Anonymous* (commonly known as the Big Book), now in its Fourth Edition, as well as in *Twelve Steps and Twelve Traditions, Living Sober,* and other books. Information on AA can also be found on AA's website at www.aa.org, or by writing to:

Alcoholics Anonymous
Box 459
Grand Central Station
New York, NY 10163

For local resources, check your local telephone directory under "Alcoholics Anonymous." Four pamphlets, "This is A.A.," "Is A.A. For You?," "44 Questions," and "A Newcomer Asks" are also available from AA.